THE
TRIANGLE

The Truth Behind the World's
Most Enduring Mystery

MIKE BARA

Adventures Unlimited Press

The Triangle
by Mike Bara

Copyright © 2019

All Rights Reserved

ISBN 13: 978-1-948803-06-9

Published by:
Adventures Unlimited Press
One Adventure Place
Kempton, Illinois 60946 USA
auphq@frontiernet.net

www.AdventuresUnlimitedPress.com

THE TRIANGLE

MIKE BARA

Adventures Unlimited Press

Acknowledgements

I would like to acknowledge the following beings and creatures that supported me in the creation of this work: My brother Dave, my publisher David Hatcher Childress, all the folks at History and Prometheus, Lori Moriarty, the team at Big Fish, and all my friends and fans on social media. Finally, Aurora, Miss Fluffy-Muffy, Barkley, Sebastian and Khaleesi. I love you all.

Other books by Mike Bara:
Ancient Aliens and JFK
Hidden Agenda
Ancient Aliens and Secret Societies
Ancient Aliens on the Moon
Ancient Aliens on Mars
Ancient Aliens on Mars II
The Choice
Dark Mission (with Richard Hoagland)

TABLE OF
CONTENTS

Dedication

This book is dedicated to all the tireless Bermuda Triangle
researchers who have worked so hard over the decades to bring
these many cases to life.

See Mike Bara at:

MikeBara.Blogspot.com

THE TRIANGLE

The Truth Behind the World's Most Enduring Mystery

A formation of TBM Avengers identical to the group that disappeared in 1945.

Introduction

For decades, no single place has intrigued the world more than the baffling mystery that is the Bermuda Triangle, also known as the Devil's Triangle. Hundreds of ships, planes and yachts have disappeared in the dark, mysterious waters between Bermuda and Florida, far more than in any other part of the world. Ships have vanished without a trace only to magically reappear years later in good order but minus their crews, almost as if the intervening years had not even passed—for them. Yachts and sea liners have gone missing in good weather with no explanation. Pilots have

An illustration of the island of Atlantis with a high mountain to the north.

reported bizarre problems with their instruments as compasses and guidance systems have spun inexplicably out of control over the shadowy waters of the Triangle. Entire squadrons of military aircraft have disappeared off of radarscopes in clear weather and with no forewarning.

Others have experienced strange magnetic anomalies and otherworldly encounters with mysterious craft and unrecognizable energetic fields. Explanations range from alien encounters to rogue waves to twisting and unnatural funnel spouts caused by submerged technology left over from the days of Atlantis.

We will investigate these and other mysteries of the Bermuda Triangle in these pages. We will find out what really happened to Flight 19, the Navy training flight that last reported "they look like they're from outer space" over the Triangle. We will examine the undersea ruins of a lost civilization just off the island of Cuba and examine the Bimini Road that leads directly into the deep waters of the Triangle.

We'll look the case of the *Cotopaxi*, the ore ship lost at sea only to apparently reappear decades later off the coast of Cuba, far beyond where it was last sighted in the Triangle's maritime shipping lanes. These and other enigmatic cases will be stripped open and laid bare before the light of history as the reader is carried on a journey to the world's most frightening and impenetrable mystery—The Bermuda Triangle.

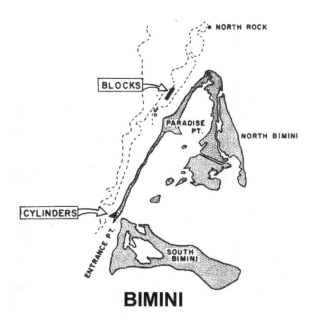

BIMINI

A photo of the pillow-shaped blocks near the north shore of Bimini island in the Bahamas. Structures at Bimini are among a number of mysterious underwater structures within the area of the Bermuda Triangle.

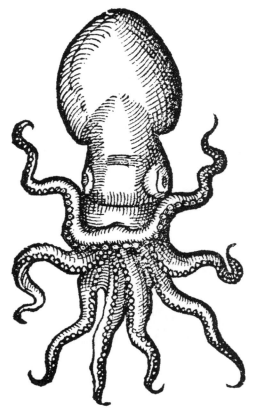

Early mariners feared an attack by the Kraken.

Chapter 1

The Triangle

The world-famous "Bermuda Triangle," also known in some circles as the "Devil's Triangle," first pushed its way into the collective consciousness in the 1970s, just shortly after the Ancient Astronauts craze stimulated by Erich von Däniken's 1968 book *Chariots of the Gods?* The Triangle was described as a vast swath of ocean in the Atlantic/Caribbean where many hundreds of ships, planes and small yachts had mysteriously disappeared or been found drifting without explanation. Two of the most famous books that popularized the tale of the Triangle at the time were Charles Berlitz' *The Bermuda Triangle* and Richard Winer's *The Devil's Triangle*, both published in 1974.

The exact boundaries of the Triangle are frequently in dispute, with some saying that it is strictly limited to the off-kilter equilateral triangle formed by connecting Miami, Bermuda and Puerto Rico. Others argue that the area of high strangeness is actually more trapezoidal and extends much farther out to sea, encompassing the wide Sargasso Sea and stretching halfway across the Atlantic Ocean.

In a 1968 book titled *This Baffling World*, author John Godwin suggested that the boundaries of the Triangle were actually a square that was defined by a line drawn from Bermuda to the Virginia coast in the north, and in the south by the Islands of Cuba, Hispaniola, and Puerto Rico. Vincent Gaddis, author of *Invisible Horizons,* is probably the one responsible for the now accepted boundaries, drawing its triangular form roughly within a line from Florida to Puerto Rico, another from Puerto Rico to Bermuda, and a third line back to Florida through the Bahamas. Author Ivan T. Sanderson, who dealt with the Triangle in his book *Invisible Residents* (Adventures Unlimited Press) and a host of articles in

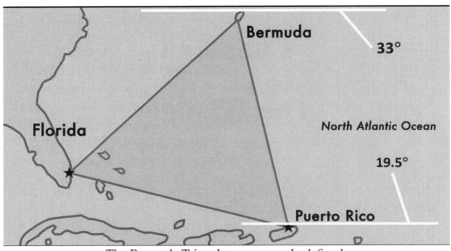

The Bermuda Triangle as commonly defined.

various forms, argued that it was actually an ellipse or lozenge shape. He also added that there were at least a dozen other of these "Devil's Triangles" spaced equally throughout the world including Japan's infamous "'Devil's Sea.'" John W. Spencer, author of *The Bermuda Triangle-UFO Connection,* suggested that the Triangle followed the continental shelf. He claimed that it started at a point off Virginia and went south following the American coast past Florida and continued around the Gulf of Mexico. Even the United States Coast Guard, which argues the Triangle is a myth, once identified its location and boundaries in a form letter numbered 5720 from the Seventh Coast Guard District:

> The Bermuda or Devil's Triangle is an imaginary area located off the southeastern Atlantic coast of the United States, which is noted for a high incidence of unexplained losses of ships, small boats, and aircraft. The apexes of the triangle are generally accepted to be Bermuda, Miami, Florida, and San Juan, Puerto Rico. There are many marine or aeronautical authorities who would observe that it is perfectly natural for planes, ships, or yachts to disappear in an area where there is so much sea and air travel, subject to sudden storms and the multiple possibilities of navigational mistakes and accidents. These same authorities are likely to make the comment that the Bermuda Triangle does

not exist at all, and that the very term is a misnomer, a manufactured mystery for the diversion of the curious and imaginative reader.[1]

History shows that decades before these suggestions of unusual disappearances in what is now known as the Bermuda Triangle took hold in the 1970s, the mystery first appeared in a September 17, 1950 Associated Press article published in *The Miami Herald* by Edward Van Winkle Jones titled "Sea's Puzzles Still Baffle Men in Pushbutton Age."[2] It told the story of the *Sandra*, a 350-foot freighter that sailed with a crew of a dozen men from Miami to Savannah, Georgia, where it took on a cargo of 300 tons of insecticide bound for Venezuela. It never arrived. Even though the ship was well equipped with radios, no distress signal was ever heard or unusual weather ever reported. The article also discussed the case of a passenger plane carrying 32 "men and women and two babies" that boarded in San Juan, Puerto Rico and flew uneventfully almost 1,000 miles toward its destination of Miami on December 27, 1948. At 4 A.M. the Miami tower received a message that the plane was less than 50 miles from the airport, at which point it simply disappeared. An extensive land, sea and air search was conducted over a 300,000 square mile area, but no trace—not even an oil slick—was ever found.

The article also described the mysterious fate of a British airliner named *Star Ariel*, which left Bermuda with 20 passengers bound for Chile from its origination point in London. It disappeared and a US Navy task force that was performing maneuvers in the area broke off their mission to search for the missing plane. They found nothing. It also describes an earlier incident on January 31, 1948 in which another British plane named *Star Tiger*, an Avro 688 Tudor Mark IV propeller plane with 29 passengers aboard, simply disappeared on final approach to Bermuda after checking in several times.

The article is also significant in that it appears to be the first reference in print to the infamous Flight 19, the five naval torpedo planes which vanished in good weather somewhere off the coast of Florida in 1945. It summarized the incident thusly:

An older but more perplexing mystery is that of the five torpedo planes. They took off from the Navy's Fort Lauderdale air station on Dec. 5, 1945, for a navigational training flight. The hours passed and darkness fell. Anxious officers called to them by radio and were answered only with silence.

The hour passed when their fuel would be exhausted and search planes were sent out. Among the searchers was a big, lumbering rescue craft, a PBM with 13 men on board.

None of the five torpedo planes with the 14 crewmen were found despite the greatest search in Florida's history. Nor did the PBM rescue craft ever return.

To my knowledge this is the first time that Flight 19 was connected with an explanation involving supernatural or mysterious disappearances in the area we now call the Triangle. Two years later, *Fate* magazine published "Sea Mystery at Our

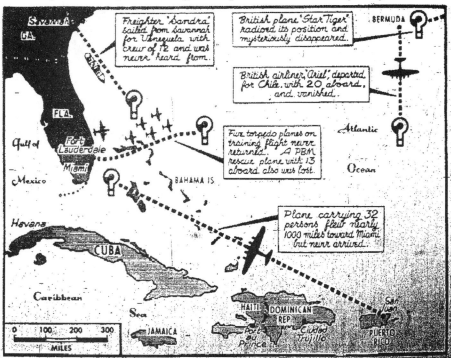

Illustration from the EW Jones article of September 15, 1950 (*Miami Herald*).

Back Door," a short article by George X. Sand covering the loss of several planes and ships, including also the loss of Flight 19. According to Wikipedia, Sand's article was apparently "the first to lay out the now-familiar triangular area where the losses took place" and also the first to suggest a supernatural element to the disappearances. Flight 19 was covered singularly in the April 1962 issue of *American Legion* magazine in an article titled "The Mystery of the Lost Patrol" by Allan W. Eckert. Eckert was the first to write that the flight leader had been heard saying, "We are entering white water, nothing seems right. We don't know where we are, the water is green, no white." He also wrote that officials at the Navy board of inquiry on Flight 19 stated that the planes "flew off to Mars."

In the February 1964 issue of *Argosy*, Vincent Gaddis wrote an article titled "The Deadly Bermuda Triangle" and argued that Flight 19 and the other cases were part of a pattern of unexplainable events in the region. In 1965, Gaddis expanded this article into a book titled *Invisible Horizons* that covered all manner of strange sea disappearances.

Whatever the agreed upon boundaries, everyone agrees that at least 100 ships, planes and small boats have simply vanished in the area without a trace, taking more than 1,000 lives along with them. Others even argue that the rate of disappearances is actually increasing, despite the fact that the seaways and airways are far more traveled than they were back in the 40s, searches are more comprehensive, records are more carefully kept and modern technologies like 2-way GPS systems and better radio equipment are available. What could be accounting for this is unclear, but we must seriously consider the supernatural explanation along with the more likely storm and rogue wave scenarios.

Some of the aerial disappearances have actually occurred while the crews were in routine radio contact with their base (in the case of the military aircraft) or final destination control towers right up until the very last minute, when they simply vanished into thin air. In some cases, these last-minute communications have taken on a far more ominous tone, with aircrews claiming they could not get their instruments to function properly. There are reports of compasses spinning, the sky turning "yellow and hazy" on clear days or the ocean suddenly foaming and churning violently while nearby ships or planes reported calm seas. Sometimes, reports are simply that the seas or sky didn't look right, with no details.

Since many of the aerial cases have been traced back to the early days of commercial aviation, a natural tendency is to blame these cases on mid-air explosions or design flaws in the early commercial aircraft of the day, like the Douglas DC-3. One example frequently cited is the case of the world's first commercial jetliner, the de Havilland DH-106 Comet.

The Comet was a marvel of modern design for its time, about the length of a modern 737 and designed to carry 36 passengers in spacious comfort in a pressurized cabin at a 40,000-foot cruising altitude. It had four powerful jet engines mounted in internal wing pods that would allow it to get passengers to faraway destinations much faster than conventional propeller-driven aircraft. It entered service in 1952.

But the Comet, operated primarily by the British Overseas Airways Corporation (BOAC), had several fatal flaws. While there were a few early incidents that raised concerns, it wasn't until 1954 that two tragic incidents exposed these drastic design errors. BOAC flight 781 out of Rome had just taken off on 10 January from Ciampino Airport en route to Heathrow Airport in London. After about 20 minutes, it simply disappeared from radar screens while the pilot was in active radio contact with the tower, and fell into the Mediterranean Sea. Subsequent rescue and recovery operations revealed that the dead had several consistent types of injuries to their heads and lungs. On April 8, a South African Airways flight took off from the same airport en route to Cairo, Egypt and while climbing through 30,000 feet about 30 minutes later, simply disintegrated in mid-air. Victims had the same types of injuries, and the Comet fleet was grounded while a board of inquiry was formed. The board concluded that both incidents were due to explosive decompression due to structural failure caused by the little-understood (at the time) phenomenon of metal fatigue. Because of the square design of the windows (among other flaws) cracks had formed at the corners, and under the stress of a pressurized cabin and takeoff maneuvers the structures had failed and the aircraft were lost. These incidents led to new regulations requiring that passenger jet windows be rounded, in order to distribute the loads more evenly, and led to other reinforcements of the aircraft structure.

The point is, airplanes back in the early days of commercial aviation had a lot of design flaws, flaws that could have led to the loss of many of these Bermuda Triangle planes in the incidents cited. The problem, though, is that the area of maximum stress on an airframe is usually at takeoff and, to a lesser extent, landing. Not in mid-air at a comfortable cruising altitude. The early propeller-driven aircraft also flew at lower altitudes, weren't always pressurized, and flew at much lower speeds, exposing their airframes to far lower stresses. So why did so many of these early aircraft simply disappear in the Triangle? And why didn't any of them leave a trace? Nothing. No life rafts, oil slicks, or wreckage are ever located.

Other aircraft, including passenger planes, have vanished while receiving landing instructions, almost as if, as has been mentioned in Naval Board of Inquiry proceedings, they had "flown through a hole in the sky." Large and small boats have also disappeared without leaving wreckage, as if they and their crews had been snatched into another dimension. Large ships, like the *Marine Sulphur Queen*, a 425-foot-long freighter, and the USS *Cyclops*, a 19,000-ton ore carrier with 309 people aboard, have also simply vanished. Other ships and boats have been found drifting within the Triangle, sometimes with an animal survivor such as a dog or canary, who could give no indication of what had happened— although in one case a talking parrot vanished along with the crew.

These unexplained disappearances have continued to the present day to the point that it now seems clear that something is very wrong in this part of the Atlantic. More recently, the trend has been toward reports from boats and planes of bizarre experiences within the boundaries of the Triangle. Almost miraculously, they survived to tell their tales. The exact cause of this unexplained peril to the planes and ships in the area is as enigmatic as ever.

In some cases, these ideas are soundly rooted in rare but conventional phenomena: massive tidal waves caused by deep ocean earthquakes, or methane emissions which rob boats of their buoyancy or cause rising fireballs that reach up and snatch planes out of the sky. In other cases, the explanations have drifted into my realm, the realm of the magical and supernatural. Space-time warps or "star gates" that form without warning and snatch planes and ships out of this plane of existence and drop them into the ghostly worlds of sea legends like the *Flying Dutchman*. Electromagnetic or gravitational vortices that interfere with instruments and electronics, which cause planes to vanish into the sea. And even sea monsters, UFOs hell-bent on abduction of passengers, and as far as desperate Atlantean cultures that need specimens for experimentation. The mystery is so pervasive that researchers are willing to entertain almost any possibility.

One of the most unusual suggestions was actually put forth by Edgar Cayce, the famous "sleeping prophet." Cayce, a psychic and healer who died in 1944, claimed that the ancient Atlanteans used crystals as a power source, similar to how early lasers used rubies as a focusing medium to increase their power output. According to Cayce, these crystal weapons were located in the Bimini area—the site of the famously controversial Bimini Road—and were subsequently sunk in the Tongue of the Ocean (a deep oceanic trench) off Andros in the Bahamas, where many of the disappearances have taken place. In Cayce's vision, an automated and abandoned crystal power source sunk a mile deep to the west of Andros was still pulsing and operating in a random pattern, exerting an influence on the modern electronic instruments of modern ships and planes.[3]

Whatever the depths of the mystery (pun intended) of the deep ocean floor of the Triangle, there can be little doubt that we know less about the depths of the oceans than we do about the depths of space. While most of us go through our daily lives confident that we know all there is to know about the boring, four billion-year-old Earth and precious little about the expanse of the vastly larger space beyond her, the opposite may be true. The deep oceans may hold more life, mystery and surprise than the vastness beyond, which we have arrogantly referred to as the "final frontier." The truth is, other than mapping the ocean floors, we know very little about them and in fact it is easier to explore the vastness of space than it is the darkest depths of the seas, simply because of the enormous pressures involved with exploring the sea bottom.

Indeed, if there is ever to be a serious attempt to catalog the full expanse of the oceans in a "Voyage to the Bottom of the Sea," entirely new technologies will have to be developed. We simply don't have alloys and metals that can survive the intense pressure experienced only a few hundred feet down, much less the miles deep trenches and holes that lead to the darkest waters of the Earth. Space, by comparison, offers many challenges, but most of those could be overcome with extant or emerging technologies. Up there, the challenge is more one of cost and return than it is of simply being able to go there. For that reason, it may take centuries longer to fully explore the ocean than it will the distant boundaries of our much larger solar system.

To be sure, we're off to a good start. Early attempts to map the ocean floors began in the 20th century. The first acoustic

The "Tongue of the Ocean" region of the Caribbean.

measurement of sea depth was made in 1914, and between 1925 and 1927 the "Meteor" expedition gathered 70,000 ocean depth measurements using an echo sounder, surveying the Mid-Atlantic ridge. The Great Global Rift, running along the Mid Atlantic Ridge, was discovered by Maurice Ewing and Bruce Heezen in 1953. In 1954 a mountain range under the Arctic Ocean was found by the Arctic Institute of the USSR. In the 1950s, Auguste Piccard invented the bathyscaphe, a deep water diving bell, and used the bathyscaphe *Trieste* to investigate the ocean's depths. The United States nuclear submarine *Nautilus* made the first journey under the ice to the North Pole in 1958. In 1962 the FLIP (Floating Instrument Platform), a 355-foot (108 m) spar buoy, was first deployed. The theory of seafloor spreading was developed in 1960 by Harry Hammond Hess, and the Deep Ocean Drilling Program started in 1966. Deep sea vents were discovered in 1977 by Jack Corliss and Robert Ballard in the submersible DSV *Alvin*, and were found to contain a wide variety of "extremophiles," deep sea creatures that were so different from other life on Earth they might as well be aliens.

We already know the deep abyssal plains and the adjoining submerged canyons contain many unusual and unexpected life forms. One of them that most of us have heard of is the supposedly "extinct" creature known as the coelacanth, a prehistoric fish with residual limbs. Thought to be extinct since the end of the Late

An old print of a ship encountering a sea serpent off Greenland in 1734.

Early mariners feared an attack by the Kraken.

Cretaceous era, the coelacanth was discovered to be very much alive and well in the Indian Ocean in 1938. This four-legged bluefish flourished about 60 million years ago, but mostly vanished in the fifth extinction about 65 million years ago. Its last fossilized specimen, before the live one was found, had been dated at 18 million years BC.

So it is against this background of mysterious pre-history that we have to consider other stories and explanations about the Triangle's dangers. We have to seriously look at ideas and explanations that we might otherwise simply dismiss as tall tales of the type that fishermen and sailors often have told over the centuries: the possibility of sea monsters.

Detailed accounts from reliable observers, many of whom had nothing to gain and much to lose in making a "sea serpent" report, have sketched or described sea creatures which resemble very much in structure the Pliocene monosaurus or ichthyosaurus, apparently still alive and well in the abyssal deep. On several occasions these creatures have been observed not just by one, but by *hundreds* of witnesses as they approached beaches and harbors situated at points varying from Tasmania to Massachusetts. The Loch Ness Monster, affectionately called "Nessie" by the local Scots, and regularly although indistinctly filmed and photographed, may be a smaller version of these giant "fish lizards," as their Greek name, Ichthyosaurus, is translated. If the coelacanth can survive 65 million years in virtual anonymity, why couldn't Nessie?

23

Other stories of unusual and strange sea creatures of potentially enormous size have emerged over the years. Anton Bruun, a Danish oceanographer, reported that he once observed a 6-foot-long eel-like tadpole brought up by a trawler. If the larval-like creature grew to an adult size in proportion to other such life forms that exist on a smaller scale, it would grow to be *72 feet long*, an extraordinary size for a previously unknown sea creature.

For centuries, seamen have told the tales of the giant squid, an enormous carnivore sometimes called the Kraken, that has attacked ships and boats in the open seas. Although said to have originated in the north Atlantic between Norway and Greenland, tales of the massive 40 to 50 foot creatures in Caribbean waters began to appear in the 1800s. Although no actual specimen of the giant squid has ever been found, skeletal remains have been found in approximately that size.

The descriptions of the Kraken are terrifying, with old Norse tales as far back as the 13th century describing a squid-like creature "as big as an island" with a wake that could swallow a dozen ships easily. "It is said that if (the creature's arms) were to lay hold of the largest man-of-war, they would pull it down to the bottom." Swedish author Jacob Wallenberg described the Kraken in the 1781 work Min son på galejan ("My son on the galley"):

An illustration of the Gloucester sea serpent of 1817.

Kraken, also called the Crab-fish, which is not that huge, for heads and tails counted, he is no larger than our Öland is wide [i.e., less than 16 km] ...He stays at the sea floor, constantly surrounded by innumerable small fishes, who serve as his food and are fed by him in return: for his meal, (if I remember correctly what E. Pontoppidan writes,) lasts no longer than three months, and another three are then needed to digest it. His excrements nurture in the following an army of lesser fish, and for this reason, fishermen plumb after his resting place... Gradually, Kraken ascends to the surface, and when he is at ten to twelve fathoms, the boats had better move out of his vicinity, as he will shortly thereafter burst up, like a floating island, spurting water from his dreadful nostrils and making ring waves around him, which can reach many miles. Could one doubt that this is the Leviathan of Job?

Even in more modern times, stories of giant sea squids and sea monsters have been taken seriously. The so-called "Gloucester sea serpent" was reportedly seen around and off the coast of Gloucester, Massachusetts and the Cape Ann area. The heyday of sightings began in August 1817 and continued into 1818-19. The earliest alleged sighting of such a creature off Cape Ann was recorded in 1638 by John Josselyn. Occasional sightings continued over the

Another illustration of the Gloucester sea serpent.

centuries and into the 20th century. The creature was described as more resembling the Loch Ness Monster than a giant sea squid, but the spate of 1817-19 sightings caused the Linnaean Society of New England to investigate. Members of the society out on boats reportedly came within 140 yards of a creature that they say resembled the descriptions of the other sightings. The residents of Gloucester later located a small black snake on a beach with humps, which they believed was the offspring of the serpent. The Society's analysis was published in a pamphlet which announced it was a new species which they dubbed "Scoliophis Atlanticus." After 1819, the creature was not seen again.

We know today from more extensive studies of the deep seas that strange creatures exist where common belief suggested that no life could exist. "Extremophiles," microbial or simple life forms that lived in ocean bottom vents of extreme heat or deep in hot springs in environments toxic to more complex forms of life, shocked biologists when they were first discovered. According to astrophysicist Steinn Sigurdsson, "There are viable bacterial spores that have been found that are 40 million years old on Earth—and we know they're very hardened to radiation." Some bacteria were found living in the cold and dark in a lake buried a half-mile deep under the ice in Antarctica, and in the Marianas Trench, the deepest place in Earth's oceans. Some microorganisms have been found thriving inside rocks up to 1,900 feet (580 m) below the sea floor under 8,500 feet of ocean off the coast of the northwestern United States. According to one of the researchers, "You can find microbes everywhere—they're extremely adaptable to conditions, and survive wherever they are." A key to extremophile adaptation is their amino acid composition, affecting their protein folding ability under particular conditions.[4]

Some of these creatures, such as the microscopic Tardigrades, are exceedingly more complex and, while small, are terrifying to look at and tough as nails. If these sea creatures were somehow scaled up to large enough sizes, either through concealed evolutionary processes or nuclear mutation—like in the Godzilla movies—they could conceivably present a threat to maritime traffic and possibly account for some of the most famous Triangle cases. But to this point, there is no evidence of that. Sea monsters

Close-ups of the terrifying Tardigrade creatures.

remain a possible, though unlikely explanation for the mystery of the Triangle.

Some argue that there are many regions of tempestuous weather and aerial and maritime disappearances that are just as active as the Triangle, and therefore there is nothing exceptional about the rate of disappearances in the Triangle at all. Lawrence David Kusche, author of *The Bermuda Triangle Mystery: Solved* (1975), was particularly harsh in his assessments that there was no mystery to the Triangle. He argued that many claims of the early writers were often exaggerated, dubious or unverifiable. Kusche's research revealed a number of inaccuracies and inconsistencies between Berlitz's accounts and statements from eyewitnesses, participants, and others involved in the initial incidents. Kusche also noted cases where what he considered "pertinent" information went unreported. Kusche further argued that a large percentage of the incidents that sparked allegations of the Triangle's mysterious influence actually occurred well outside it, which is interesting, since the exact boundaries of the "Triangle" are frequently debated. In his book he described the Caribbean as an "area frequented by tropical cyclones," and claimed the number of disappearances that did occur were neither disproportionate, unlikely, nor mysterious. He cited the number of incidents in the South China Sea as an example, since it was also an area of the ocean that saw violent storms and typhoons.[5]

An old print of one of the many demons of the sea.

But this in itself is very interesting: Why is it that the South China Sea and the Bermuda Triangle are the two most active regions for unexplained disappearances of ships and planes, and they occupy essentially the same location 180° around the circumference of the Earth? The Triangle lies basically between 19.5 degrees North and 33 degrees North in the Western hemisphere and the South China Sea takes up the same real estate exactly halfway around the globe. Commonly, hurricanes and typhoons are blamed on rising sea temperatures due to intense summer heat carried by ocean currents. But, if that is the case, shouldn't those storms form more readily in the equatorial regions, where the Earth is hottest, rather than 20-33° farther North, where the oceans should be considerably cooler?

The answer is yes. So why don't these storms form with more variation and where the water is considerably warmer? Some say it has to do with wind patterns, storm flows and ocean currents. But, I strongly suggest—and will show later in this volume—there's more to it than that, and it involves a new concept of physical laws sent to us by inhabitants of another, and perhaps alien, highly advanced civilization.

Some authors, like Berlitz, viewed the dilemma presented by the Triangle this way:

There is a difference, however, between these multiple mysteries which may eventually be solved (and which meanwhile are intriguing to contemplate) and the one posed by the Bermuda Triangle, which introduces an element of danger to the traveler. It is true, of course, that numerous planes fly over the Triangle every day, that large and small ships sail its waters, and that countless travelers visit the area every year without incident. Besides, ships and planes have been lost at sea and continue to be lost in all the world's seas and oceans for a variety of reasons (and we must remember to differentiate between "lost at sea," which suggests the finding of wreckage or some identifiable flotsam, and "disappeared," which implies none at all), but in no other area have the unexplained disappearances been so numerous, so well recorded, so sudden, and attended by such unusual circumstances, some of which push the element of coincidence to the borders of impossibility.

That, definitively, is what I plan to reveal within these pages. That while stories of sea monsters, unexplained whirlpools, rogue waves and unexplained electrical phenomena have been with us since the dawn of the sailing age, the Triangle represents a mystery far more intriguing, far more challenging, and far more enigmatic. It represents in fact the Holy Grail of paranormal tests. If a cause, effect or even a strong case for reality can be made, then many other mysteries of the world are on the table: ghosts, bigfoot, UFOs, aliens themselves, perhaps even the answers to the cattle mutilation experiments. Solving the mystery of the Triangle can lead to so many more answers.

If only we knew where to start.

My preference, as always, is to start at the beginning.

1 *The Bermuda Triangle*, Charles Berlitz, Avon Books ISBN-13: 978-0380004652
2 http://www.physics.smu.edu/pseudo/BermudaTriangle/evwjones.html
3 The Bermuda Triangle, Charles Berlitz, Avon Books ISBN-13: 978-0380004652
4 https://en.wikipedia.org/wiki/Extremophile
5 https://en.wikipedia.org/wiki/Bermuda_Triangle

Chapter 2

Flight 19

There can be no doubt that the case of Flight 19, the disappearance of five Navy aircraft on a training run on December 5, 1945, gave birth to the mythology of the Bermuda Triangle. It is without question the most intriguing aviation mystery of the 20th century at least, not even rivaled until the disappearance of Malaysia Airlines flight MH370 in March of 2017, which had nothing to do with the Bermuda Triangle (although, to be fair, it did occur in or near the South China Sea "Triangle" we discussed in Chapter 1). Like many other classic Bermuda Triangle mysteries, it occurred in broad daylight, in good weather, and involved an experienced crew. But it is unique for several reasons. For one, it was not an isolated incident, as another search plane sent out to look for the missing planes also disappeared without a trace. For another, it is the first such incident which seemed to involve a possible alien component in its mythos.

It also had something of a role in giving the Bermuda Triangle its name. The initial mission flight plan (which may or may not have been followed) was actually a triangle pattern, taking off from the Fort Lauderdale Naval Air Station, then flying 60 miles east out to sea. The flight of the five aircraft was then to turn north for 40 miles before turning back to Fort Lauderdale and landing back on the Naval Air Station runway. Investigators and reporters noticed at the time that the apex of this proposed flight plan was in direct alignment with Bermuda, because even then the area around Bermuda was known for a number of fairly inexplicable aerial and sea disappearances.[1]

But Flight 19 was different, a sea mystery at a whole other level because it involved military aircraft, experienced pilots and a massive search and rescue operation that only added to the mystery instead of offering a possible explanation. It is the only

31

case I know of where not only were there multiple military aircraft lost in the Triangle, but additionally, even more military aircraft sent out to look for them *also* disappeared without a trace. Flight 19 was on a whole new level of bizarreness, one that would put it forever into the annals of UFO lore.

Flight 19 was supposed to be a simple bombing run, a training mission to practice attacking ships at sea with propeller torpedo bombers as had been done multiple times in the raging sea battles of the Pacific theater in World War II, which had obviously just ended. The Navy viewed it as a necessity to keep their pilots sharply honed in these skills and there were a lot of small bomber wings stationed at various bases in Florida postwar.

The training flight was supposed to be initiated from Naval Air Station Fort Lauderdale, an airfield of the United States Navy just outside Fort Lauderdale, Florida. In 1942, the US Navy selected Merle Fogg Airport in Fort Lauderdale to expand into a naval air station for both pilot and enlisted aircrew training (i.e., gunners, radiomen) in Grumman TBF Avenger torpedo bombers flown by carrier-based US Navy flight crews and by land-based US Marine Corps flight crews ashore. Additional facilities were used to train aircraft maintenance and other ground crew support for the TBF and TBM series aircraft. Interestingly, among the Avenger pilots who graduated NAS Fort Lauderdale was former President George H. W. Bush, from a class in 1943.[2]

Several airfields in the immediate vicinity of NAS Fort Lauderdale were commissioned as Navy satellite airfields, also known as outlying fields (OLF). Several of these fields continue in operation today as civilian airports, such as Fort Lauderdale Executive Airport and North Perry Airport. Naval Air Station Banana River is now Patrick Air Force Base, and flights from those fields took part in the search for Flight 19. Today, Patrick AFB is now home to the 4th Space Wing, among others.

The torpedo bomber training was difficult and dangerous. From 1942 through 1946, 94 pilots lost their lives while serving at NAS Fort Lauderdale. The crews of Flight 19, 14 men including experienced pilots and an experienced squadron commander, are among those 94. Their disappearance, among the last of the 94 fatalities (or presumed dead) listed as originating from the base,

Naval Air Station Banana River in the mid-1940s, now Patrick Air Force Base.

may have had a role in the decommissioning of the facility. About a year later, citing the obsolescence of the Avenger aircraft and the lack of "hot" war enemies, the Navy closed the base and it was turned over to the local government of Broward County, Florida for use as a civilian airport. Today the facility is known as Fort Lauderdale-Hollywood International Airport.

But up until that time it was still an active base and Flight 19 was one of many training missions that flew daily from the airfield. Flight 19 was manned by five pilots, all officers, and nine enlisted crew members. The enlisted men were assigned two to each plane, normally making a complement of 15 men, but on the day of the disappearance the flight was short one man who had requested that he be removed from flight certification because of a recent promotion. Instead of canceling the training mission, the flight of five Navy Grumman TBM-3 Avenger torpedo bombers simply went out a man short. In the Navy, that's what you did. Each of the five planes was loaded with enough fuel to enable it to cruise over a thousand miles round trip.

The day was exceptionally good for flying. The temperature was a perfect 65 degrees, the sun was shining and there were only a few scattered clouds and a moderate northeast wind. Pilots who had flown earlier the same day reported ideal flying weather. Flight time was calculated as two hours for this specific mission.

The bomber group was commanded by Lieutenant Charles C. Taylor, USNR, flying tail number FT-28 and crewed by George Devlin, AOM3c, USNR and Walter R. Parpart, ARM3c, USNR. The plane was US Navy Bureau Number 23307. The second plane, tail number FT-36, was piloted by Captain E. J. Powers, USMC, and crewed by Staff Sergeant Howell O. Thompson, USMCR and Sergeant George R. Paonessa, USMC. The Bureau Number was 46094. The third plane, FT-3, was piloted by Ensign Joseph T. Bossi, USNR and crewed by S1c Herman A. Thelander, USNR and S1c Burt E. Baluk, JR., USNR. The Bureau Number was 45714. The fourth plane, FT-117 was piloted by Captain George W. Stivers, USMC and crewed by Pvt Robert P. Gruebel, USMCR, and Sergeant Robert F. Gallivan, USMC. The Bureau Number of this aircraft was 73209. The fifth plane, tail number FT-81, was the plane with only one crew member and was flown by 2nd Lieutenant Forrest J. Gerber, USMCR and crewed by PFC William E. Lightfoot, USMCR. The Bureau Number for this plane was 46325.

Many of the pilots had experience flying over the waters off Florida. The group leader, Charles Carroll Taylor (born October 25, 1917), had over 2,500 hours flying time in an Avenger torpedo bomber and had graduated from Naval Air Station Corpus Christi in February, 1942. He became a flight instructor in October of that year. His trainee pilots each had 300 hours total flight experience, and 60 flight hours in the Avenger. Taylor had completed a combat tour in the Pacific theatre as torpedo bomber pilot on the aircraft carrier USS *Hancock* and had recently arrived from NAS Miami where he had also been a VTB instructor. The student pilots had recently completed other training missions in the area where the flight was to take place.

The planes started taking off at 2 PM local time and by 2:10 PM they were all airborne. Both pilots and crews were experienced airmen and there was no reason to expect anything of an unusual nature to happen during the routine mission of Flight 19. During preflight checks it was discovered that the planes were all missing clocks. Navigation of the route was intended to teach dead reckoning principles, which involved calculating among other things elapsed time. The apparent lack of timekeeping equipment was not a cause for concern as it was assumed each man had his own watch. Takeoff was scheduled for 13:45 local time, but the late arrival of Taylor delayed departure until 14:10. By this time, the weather at NAS Fort Lauderdale had shifted and was described as "favorable, sea state moderate to rough."[3] Taylor was supervising the mission, and a trainee pilot had the role of leader out front.

The exercise had three key "waypoints" along the flight path and also the practice bombing run on an abandoned sea hulk. Called "Naval Air Station, Fort Lauderdale, Florida, navigation problem No. 1," the plan was to fly on heading 091° (almost due east) for 56 nautical miles until reaching Hen and Chickens Shoals, where the low level bombing practice was carried out. The flight was then to continue on that heading for another 67 nautical miles before turning onto a course of 346° for 73 nautical miles, in the process over-flying Grand Bahama Island. The next scheduled turn was to a heading of 241° to fly 120 nautical miles at the end of which the exercise was completed and the Avengers would turn slightly left to then return to NAS Ft. Lauderdale. After takeoff, subsequent radio conversations between the pilots were overheard by the base and other aircraft in the area.[4]

The practice bombing operation is known to have been carried out because at about 15:00 (3 PM local time) one of the pilots requested and was given permission to drop his last bomb. Forty minutes later, another flight instructor, Lieutenant Robert F. Cox in FT-74, forming up with his group of students for the same mission, received an unidentified transmission and had a direct conversation with Powers. An unidentified Flight 19 crew member asked Powers, one of the students, for his compass reading. Powers replied: "I don't know where we are. We must have got lost after that last turn." Cox then transmitted; "This is FT-74, plane or boat calling 'Powers' please identify yourself so someone can help you." The response after a few moments was a request from the others in the Cox flight for suggestions. FT-74 tried again and a man identified as FT-28 (Taylor) came on. "FT-28, this is FT-74, what is your trouble?" "Both of my compasses are out," Taylor replied, "and I am trying to find Fort Lauderdale, Florida. I am over land but it's broken. I am sure I'm in the Keys but I don't know how far down and I don't know how to get to Fort Lauderdale."

FT-74 informed Fort Lauderdale NAS that the aircraft were lost and then advised Taylor to put the sun on his port wing and fly north up the coast to Fort Lauderdale. Base operations then asked if the flight leader's aircraft was equipped with a standard "YG" (IFF transmitter), which could be used to triangulate the flight's position, but the message was not acknowledged by FT-28. (Later he would indicate that his transmitter was activated.) Instead, at 16:45 (4:45 PM), FT-28 radioed: "We are heading 030 degrees for 45 minutes, then we will fly north to make sure we are not over the Gulf of Mexico."

During this time no bearings could be made on the flight, and the IFF (Identification Friend or Foe) could not be picked up. Taylor was told to broadcast on 4805 kHz. This order was not acknowledged so he was asked to switch to 3000 kHz, the search and rescue frequency. Taylor replied, "I cannot switch frequencies. I must keep my planes intact."

At 16:56, Taylor was again asked to turn on his transmitter for "YG" if he had one. He did not acknowledge but a few minutes

NAS Ft. Lauderdale training squadron markings of FT-28, Lt. Taylor's Avenger

later he was heard to advise his flight "Change course to 090 degrees [due east] for 10 minutes." About the same time someone in the flight said "Dammit, if we could just fly west we would get home; head west, dammit." This difference of opinion later led to questions about why the students did not simply head west on their own. It has been argued that this can simply be attributed to military discipline, but it may have cost the men their lives. As the weather deteriorated slightly, radio contact became intermittent, and it was believed that the five aircraft were actually by that time more than 200 nautical miles out to sea east of the Florida peninsula. Taylor radioed: "We'll fly 270 degrees west until landfall or running out of gas" and requested a weather check at 17:24 (5:24 PM local time).

By 17:50 several land-based radio stations had triangulated Flight 19's position as being within a 100 nautical mile radius of 29°N, 79°W. Flight 19 was north of the Bahamas and well off the coast of central Florida, but nobody transmitted this information on an open, repetitive basis. At 18:04, Taylor radioed to his flight "Holding 270, we didn't fly far enough east, we may as well just turn around and fly east again." By that time, the weather had deteriorated even more and the sun had since set. Around 18:20, Taylor's last message was received. (It has also been reported that Taylor's last message was received at 19:04). He was heard saying "All planes close up tight … we'll have to ditch unless landfall … when the first plane drops below 10 gallons, we all go down together."

As it became obvious the flight was lost, air bases, aircraft, and merchant ships were alerted. A Consolidated PBY Catalina departed after 18:00 to search for Flight 19 and guide them back if they could be located. After dark, two Martin PBM Mariner flying boats originally scheduled for their own training flights were diverted to perform square pattern searches in the area west of 29°N, 79°W. At 19:27 (7:27 PM local time). One of the Mariners took off from NAS Banana River to search for the planes in the area north of the Bahamas where flight controllers suspected the Flight had ditched. US Navy Squadron Training No. 49 PBM-5 Bureau No 59225 called in a routine radio message at 19:30 and was never heard from again. The tower had received the signal from Lieutenant Come, one of the officers on the plane.

He reported that there were "strong winds" above 6,000 feet but did not expect them to present a serious challenge to the search. This contradicts commonly cited "reports" that the weather was bad off the coast earlier in the day, creating white water conditions. The PBM Mariner did not encounter such winds until it was over a mile up, and they could not have accounted for the loss of the plane. A short while later, the other rescue planes received the message that they were now looking for six planes instead of five. The PBM Mariner and the 13 souls aboard her had now also disappeared.

According to some reports, the aircraft exploded shortly after takeoff. The evidence for this is somewhat flimsy but bears looking at. It was reported that at 21:15 (9:15 PM local time), the tanker SS *Gaines Mills* reported it had observed flames from an apparent explosion leaping 100 feet high and burning for 10 minutes, at position 28.59°N 80.25°W. Captain Shonna Stanley reported unsuccessfully searching for survivors through a pool of oil and aviation gasoline. The escort carrier USS *Solomons* also reported losing radar contact with an aircraft at the same position and time. It was assumed to be the now missing PBM Mariner, but no wreckage, bodies or other evidence was ever found to confirm or support this assumption. The official report[5] states:

54. That at 2115R on 5 December 1945 the SS *Gaines Mills* reported as follows:

At 0050 G. M. T. observed burst of flames, apparently explosion, leaping flames 100 feet high burning ten minutes. Position 28 degrees, 59 minutes north, 80 degrees 25 minutes west. At present, passing through big pool of oil at 0119 G. M. T. Stopped, circled area using search lights, looking for survivors. None found.

55. That USS *Solomons* CVE-67 dispatched at 06127 reported as follows: 'Our air search radar showed plane after takeoff from Banana River last night joining with another plane, then separation and proceeding on course 045 degrees at exact time SS *Gaines Mills* sighted flames in exact spot the above plane disappeared from the radar

screen and never reappeared.

56. That concentrated search operations from 6 December to 10 December 1945, inclusive, by surface and aircraft in the area of the reported explosion failed to reveal any debris of the missing PBM or evidence of its crew.

Now, the reason this all seems flimsy to me is the fact that for one thing, the timing is all wrong. The PBM took off at 7:27 PM,

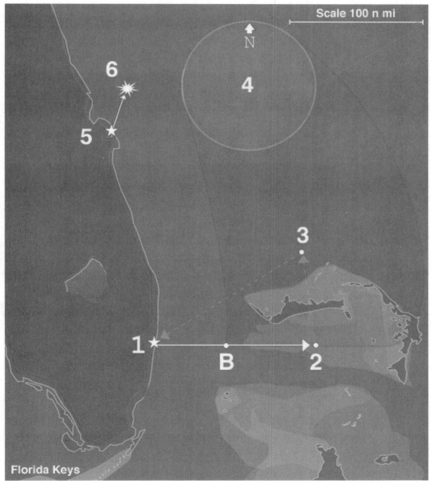

The assumed flight path of Flight 19: 1. NAS Ft. Lauderdale. B. The bombing target. 2. Where they were supposed to turn north. 3. Where they were supposed to turn back home. 5. Take off point of the PBY Catalina search plane. 6. Possible location of "explosion."

The PBM Mariner that disappeared looking for Flight 19. (Naval Air Station Fort Lauderdale Museum)

radioed in three minutes later, and was never heard from again. Flights of this type are required to regularly check in with flight control towers and report their position, altitude and bearing. They never did. The explosion that was reported was at approximately 9:15 PM over an *hour and a half* later. Why didn't they report on their position in that entire time? What happened in those intervening 105 minutes to that PBM flight that made it completely silent and except for the USS *Solomons* report, apparently radar invisible?

There is also the problem with the visual report itself. The "explosion" is reported as being only "100 feet" in the air, far too low for an aircraft of that type to be conducting a search. It is also highly doubtful that the *Solomons'* radar could have tracked the Mariner at such a low altitude. A further oddity is that it supposedly burned for over 10 minutes. The explosion of an aircraft would be over far more quickly, probably burning for less than two or three minutes, at best, and would leave flaming debris that would have easily been recovered by the SS *Gaines Mills*. Why wasn't it? And finally, airplanes simply do not explode in midair all by themselves. Something external must have caused the PBM explosion, if one even took place. What was it?

Out of 1,366 PBM Mariners built, only five were ever lost (including the one searching for Flight 19) and none of those, save the one that took off from NAS Banana River, was ever alleged to have "exploded." Conventional reports claim that the PBM Mariners were "notoriously accident prone" and were nicknamed "The flying gas tank." The reality is that they had few accidents. And the implication of some debunkers that one of the crew simply "forgot" that he was on a plane nicknamed the "flying gas tank" and lit up a cigarette is absurd. The fact remains to this day that no one has a clue what happened to the PBM, much less Flight 19.

An investigation was immediately launched into the disappearance of Flight 19 and the PBM and a 500-page Navy board of investigation report was published a few months later. It revealed new details and came to the following conclusions:

1. Flight leader Lt. Charles C. Taylor had mistakenly believed that the small islands he passed over were the Florida

Keys, that his flight was over the Gulf of Mexico, and that heading northeast would take them to Florida. It was determined that Taylor had passed over the Bahamas as scheduled, and he did in fact lead his flight to the northeast over the Atlantic. The report noted that some subordinate officers did likely know their approximate position as indicated by radio transmissions stating that flying west would result in reaching the mainland.

2. Taylor was not at fault because the compasses stopped working.
3. The loss of PBM-5 BuNo 59225 was attributed to an explosion.

This report was subsequently amended to "cause unknown" by the Navy after Taylor's mother contended that the Navy was unfairly blaming her son for the loss of five aircraft and 14 men, when the Navy had neither the bodies nor the airplanes as evidence. Taylor was exonerated in 1947 by the Board for Correction of Naval Records, in regard to "responsibility for loss of lives and naval aircraft."[6]

All of this has led to speculation as to what actually happened to Flight 19, which can be generally summarized as follows.[7]

Had Flight 19 actually been where Taylor believed it to be, the flight would have made landfall with the Florida coastline within 20 minutes, depending on how far down they were. However, a later reconstruction of the incident showed that the islands visible to Taylor were probably the Bahamas, well northeast of the Keys, and that Flight 19 was exactly where it should have been. The board of investigation found that because of his belief that he was on a base course toward Florida, Taylor actually guided the flight farther northeast and out to sea. Further, it was general knowledge at NAS Fort Lauderdale that if a pilot ever became lost in the area to fly a heading of 270° west (or in evening hours toward the sunset if the compass had failed). By the time the flight actually turned west, they were likely so far out to sea they had already passed their aircrafts' fuel endurance. This factor combined with bad weather, and the ditching characteristics of the Avenger, meant that there was little hope of rescue, even if they had managed to stay afloat.

It is possible that Taylor overshot Castaway Cay and instead reached another land mass in southern Abaco Island. He then proceeded northwest as planned. He fully expected to find the Grand Bahama Island lying in front of him as expected. Instead, he eventually saw a land mass to his right side, the northern part of Abaco Island. Believing that this landmass to his right was the Grand Bahama Island and his compass was malfunctioning, he set a course to what he thought was southwest to head straight back to Fort Lauderdale. However, in reality this changed his course farther northwest, toward the open ocean.

To further add to his confusion, he encountered a series of islands north of Abaco Island, which look very similar to the Key West Islands. The control tower then suggested that Taylor's team should fly west, which would have taken them to the landmass of Florida eventually. Taylor headed for what he thought was west, but in reality was northwest, almost parallel to Florida.

After trying that for a while and with no land in sight, Taylor decided that it was impossible for them to fly so far west and not reach Florida. He believed that he might have been near the Florida Keys. What followed was a series of serious conversations between Taylor, his team and the control tower. Taylor was not sure whether he was near Bahama or Key West, and he was not sure which direction was which due to compass malfunction. The control tower informed Taylor that he could not be over Key West since the wind that day did not blow that way.

Some of his teammates believed that their compass was working. Taylor then set a course northeast according to their compass, which should take them to Florida if they were at Key West. When that failed, Taylor set a course west according to their compass, which should take them to Florida if they were in Bahama. If Taylor stayed this course he would have reached land before running out of fuel. However, at some point Taylor decided that he had tried going west long enough. He then once again set a course northeast, thinking they were near Key West after all. Finally, his flight ran out of fuel and may have crashed into the ocean somewhere north of Abaco Island and east of Florida.

According to a history of Flight 19 posted by the NAS Fort

Lauderdale website, other pilots who flew out of the base were mystified as to how an experienced pilot like Taylor could have gotten lost. Lt. Dave White of Hillsboro Beach, who was a Senior Flight Instructor at NASFL, remembers that fateful day, as he was playing bridge when he heard a knock on the door of his friend's house: 'It was the duty officer, and he said all flight instructors were due at the hangar at 5 AM because five planes were missing.' For the next three days, White, his assistant instructor and 20 of his students flew up and down the Florida coast at low altitudes, but they couldn't find a trace of the airmen or the wreckage. White remains mystified as he has mentioned:

> The leader was an experienced combat pilot, these were reliable planes in good condition, and it was a routine training mission. We were alerted to look around the islands and to keep searching the water for debris. *They just vanished.* We had hundreds of planes out looking, and we searched over land and water for days, and nobody ever found the bodies or any debris.

Another pilot, Frank Dailey, from Alpharetta, Georgia, a Naval Reserve Captain, flew in a PBY seaplane. He recalls that for "three days, six hours a day, they plowed up and down the whole coast of Florida, looking for wreckage but we never saw a thing."

But something happened to the planes. The question is what? Other researchers, like Charles Berlitz, have reconstructed the events of Flight 19 quite differently from the commonly repeated claims of a "compass malfunction."

According to Berlitz, at 3:15 PM, about an hour after takeoff and after the bombing run had been completed and the planes had continued east, the radioman at the Fort Lauderdale Naval Air station got the first hint that something may be amiss. The Air Station control tower personnel, who had been expecting contact from the planes regarding estimated time of arrival and landing instructions, received an unusual message from the flight leader. The record shows the following:

Flight Leader (Lieutenant Charles Taylor): Calling

Tower. This is an emergency. We seem to be off course. We cannot see land... Repeat ... We cannot see land.

    Tower: What is your position'?

    Flight Leader: We are not sure of our position. We cannot be sure just where we are... We seem to be lost.

    Tower: Assume bearing due west.

    Flight Leader: *We don't know which way is west.* Everything is wrong... Strange... We can't be sure of any direction—even the ocean doesn't look as it should...

About 15 minutes later, the senior flight instructor (Cox) at Fort Lauderdale had picked up on his radio a message from someone calling himself "Powers," one of the student flyers, requesting information about his compass readings and heard Powers say, "'I don't know where we are. We must have got lost after that last turn." The senior flight instructor was able to contact Taylor, who told him, "'Both my compasses are out. I am trying to find Fort Lauderdale... I am sure I'm in the Keys, but I don't know how far down..."

Cox then advised Taylor to fly north—with the sun on his portside—until he reached the Fort Lauderdale Naval Air Station. But he subsequently heard: "We have just passed over a small island.... No other land in sight." This was an indication that Taylor's plane was *not* over the Keys as he suspected and that the entire flight was lost. Since they were unable to see land, it followed that they weren't anywhere near the Keys.

According to the reports, it became increasingly difficult to hear messages from Flight 19 because of static caused by high sunspot activity at the time. Based on the transcripts, it appears that Flight 19 could not hear further transmissions from the tower, but the tower could hear conversations between the planes. Some of these messages referred to possible fuel shortages, including someone saying they only had fuel for 75 more miles. There were also references to 75 mile-per-hour winds, but one or both of those transmissions may have been misunderstood by the tower through the static.

But then came the unnerving if not downright eerie statement from one of the pilots that "every gyro and magnetic compass in all the planes are going crazy." According to one of the overheard transmissions, each was showing a different reading. During all this time the powerful transmitter at Fort Lauderdale was unable to make any contact with the five aircraft, although the plane-to-plane communications was reported as fairly clear.

What kind of electrical phenomenon could cause this sort of behavior from the flight instruments? The malfunction of one compass, although unlikely, is always remotely possible. But the malfunction of *all five* of the planes' compasses (and radios) is a virtual impossibility absent an external causation. It's almost as if some sort of electromagnetic cloud had enveloped Flight 19, preventing radio transmissions from getting to the planes while causing their instruments to go wild.

By this time the personnel of the base were in an understandable uproar as news spread that Flight 19 had encountered some kind of emergency. As we know rescue craft were dispatched and a search and rescue operation was launched. But what happened next was even stranger.

According to Berlitz, at 4 PM the tower got an alarming transmission that sounded like Lieutenant Taylor had turned over command to a senior Marine pilot, Captain George W. Stivers, piloting aircraft number FT-117. The static interference made it hard to make out what followed exactly, but the tower officer reported that the message sounded like something of a distress call:

> We are not sure where we are… We think we must be 225 miles northeast of base…. We must have passed over Florida and we must be in the Gulf of Mexico…

The flight leader (apparently now Stivers) then decided to turn 180 degrees in the hope of flying back over Florida, But, as they made the turn the transmission began to get fainter, indicating that they had made a wrong turn and were flying east, *away* from the Florida coast and out over the open sea. Some reports claim that the last words heard from Flight 19 were: "It looks like we are [static]. Other listeners in the tower remembered more, such as: "'Entering white water… We are completely lost…"

By this time, Cox in FT-74, had decided he knew where they were and wanted to fly out and meet them and lead them back in. He was denied permission to do so. The conventional explanation is that the weather was getting worse. But there are clues that there may have been another reason.

Another version of this dialog was reported in an issue of (now defunct) *SAGA* magazine in 1972. It tells a very different story of what was actually overheard in the tower that late afternoon. The sources are quoted as multiple local "ham radio" operators who were listening in on the transmissions between the tower, the aircraft and Cox's flight group. According to at least two witnesses who were interviewed, the hams reported that the actual dialog (Stivers responding to Cox's request to go out into the Triangle to look for Flight 19) went like this:

> Cox (to tower): "Request permission to take my [static] out to look for Powers. I think I know where they are."
> Stivers (overlapping): Entering white water... We are completely lost..."
> (Pause)
> Stivers (panicked): "It looks like they're from *outer space*! [static]. Don't come after me!"
> Tower (flight officer) to Cox: "Very definitely, no."

No jets were scrambled due to the alleged "worsening weather," this fact might actually support the *SAGA* account. Signals between the tower and Flight 19 might not have been clear, but radio transmissions between the planes, tower and Cox would certainly have been audible in other locations along the Florida coast because of the different conditions and geometry of the radio waves. The scary part is that the version overheard by the ham operators suggests that something else—something otherworldly—may have been responsible for the lost flight.

This scenario was later supported on national television in 1974 when a reporter who had covered the disappearance of Flight 19 twenty-nine years before named Art Ford came forward for the first time. He corroborated the ham radio report and the "Don't come after me... They look like they're from outer space" quote.

He said he talked to the local ham operator who overheard the transmission at the time and later corroborated it in a previously secret transcript that had been given to him by a Navy source.

Of course, the official investigation and report did not mention any of these facts or testimonies. It did however illuminate certain facts that call the semi-official narrative as to what happened into question. For instance, while no further transmissions were officially heard by either the tower or the hams after the "Don't come after me!" message, there was a report from the Miami-based Opa-Locka Naval Air Station that they received a faint message with the call letters "FT... FT..." sometime after 9 PM local time that night. "FT-28" was the call sign to Lt. Taylor's Avenger that day. The problem is this would have put the message as more than an hour after Flight 19 would have run out of fuel.

Or did it? Is it possible that Flight 19 not only encountered the same "electronic fog" that other pilots have reported in the Triangle, but also experienced some kind of time displacement as well? What if, like the case of Bruce Gernon decades later (see chapter 3), Flight 19 went "somewhere else" for a few hours, only to be redeposited back into reality with no idea where they were or what time it was, and malfunctioning electromagnetic instruments to boot?

What if...

The report also revealed just how massive the search for Flight 19 was.

Shortly after the disappearance of the PBM Mariner, the air search was called off for the night because of darkness and over concern about what had happened to the Mariner. While they hoped that the plane was simply experiencing radio problems and that it would land along with the other search planes, that hope was dashed by midnight. The Coast Guard continued to search for survivors or wreckage through the night, but found no vestige whatsoever of so much as an oil slick. At first light, a massive air, sea and land search was initiated with great haste.

At least 240 planes took off in all directions to search for any sign of the presumably crashed/ditched aircraft, with 67 additional planes from the *Solomons*. The naval task force consisted of the *Solomons*, four destroyers, at least three submarines and eight

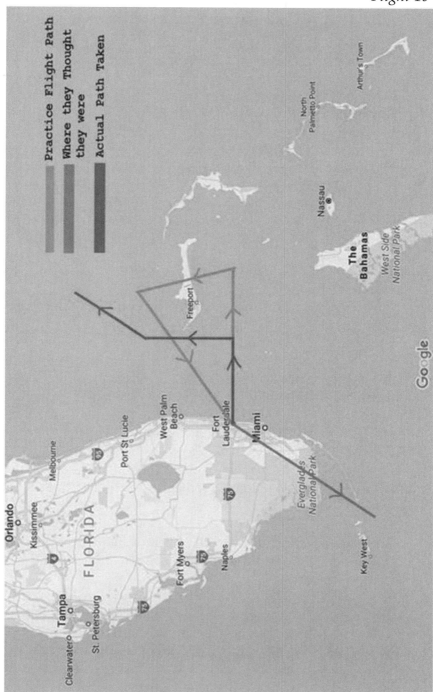

The conventional interpretation of the scheduled vs. actual flight path of Flight 19.

Coast Guard ships including a search and rescue cutter. In addition, hundreds of private planes, yachts and pleasure boats joined in the search along with additional air and seas assets from British RAF and Royal Navy forces in the Bahamas. Despite a daily average of 167 flights scouring an area of 380,000 square miles from the Gulf of Mexico to the Atlantic and Caribbean Sea at less than 500 feet, nothing was ever found. The beaches were also watched closely for wreckage, but nothing washed ashore. The search lasted over 4,100 hours in total, but found no trace of the six missing planes. No rafts, no seat cushions, not even an oil slick. They just vanished.

Once the search was called off, the official investigation was launched into high gear. The "red flare" that had been reported turned out to be from a group of revelers shooting a flare gun along a Florida beach and not the exploding Mariner. Despite this, debunkers continue to argue that an unexplained "explosion" is the explanation for the Mariner's disappearance.

The inquiry also established that no official "SOS" message was ever received from any of the lost aircraft, and that the pilots of the Avengers, at least, should have been able to survive ditching at sea. They were designed to land safely even in rough seas (which have not been established as being present in the area) and would be able to stay afloat for at least 90 seconds. The crews were trained to get out of the planes in that amount of time and deploy lifeboats, so if they ditched it seems implausible that at least one of the crew members didn't get to a boat safely.

The inquiry also established without a doubt that something caused the planes' navigation equipment to malfunction. Part of the report states:

> A radio message intercepted indicated that the planes were lost and that they were experiencing malfunctioning of their compasses.

It focused on the message referring to "white water" conditions on a calm and sunny day and the less well-referenced message that the sun "doesn't look right." The seas off the coast of Florida can occasionally produce a dense and confusing "white haze," but the conditions that day were not thought to be conducive to that being a factor in the incident. Further, it would not have affected the functioning of the gyroscopes and compasses on the aircraft, which was clearly reported. The Board debated whether to initiate a court-martial against the Instrument Officer of the day, but decided against it when they ascertained that all of the planes' instruments had been tested and were functioning as they should be prior to takeoff.

Another part of the report corroborates the odd and unexplainable malfunctioning of the instruments. Lieutenant R. H. Wirshing, assigned to the Fort Lauderdale base as a training officer like Taylor, testified that he had led a similar training mission in the same area earlier in the day, and that his flight also experienced an unexplained compass malfunction off the Florida coast and had to land at another airfield some 50 miles to the north of the FLNAS. What the source of this mysterious "electronic fog" was in the area that day has never been established, but it may play key role in unraveling the multiple mysteries of the Triangle.

Wirshing was also a personal witness to one of the stranger aspects of the saga of Flight 19; the hint that at least one of the scheduled pilots had a premonition. According to Wirshing, one of the pilots, Marine corporal Allan Kosnar, simply did not report to the flight line that day. Kosnar was quoted in the press at that time as telling them "I can't explain why, but for some strange reason

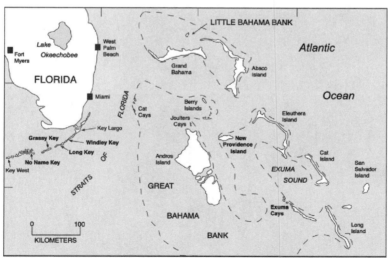

A map of southern Florida and the Bahamas.

The Triangle

I decided not to go on the flight that day." He also added that he had "a feeling" something might go wrong that day. But Wirshing claimed that Kosnar, a Guadalcanal veteran who had only four more months to serve before being discharged, had requested "several months earlier" to be relieved from flight duty.

On the day of Flight 19, Kosnar brought the matter up with Wirshing again and this time Wirshing acquiesced to the request

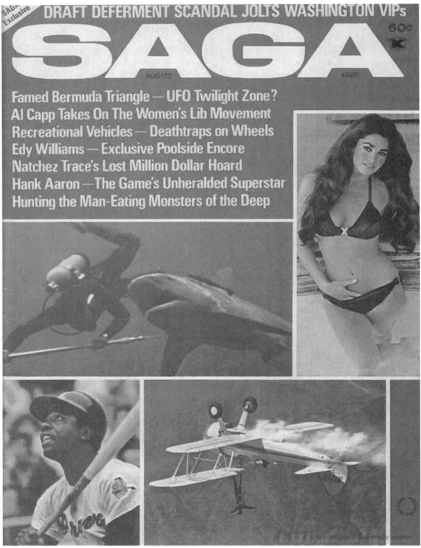

August 1972 issue of *SAGA* magazine.

and told him to report to the flight surgeon to be relieved from flight duty. Kosnar immediately did so, and according to official records, Flight 19 took off one crew member short as a result. Later, when Wirshing went to the enlisted men's barracks to look for volunteers to lead a search for the missing planes, Kosnar was present and informed Wirshing "Remember you told me to see the flight surgeon? I did, and he relieved me of flight orders. That is my flight that is lost." The problem is that according to an initial report from the flight line, the planes had gone out with *full crew complements*, implying that someone else had stepped into Kosnar's seat at the last minute. This led to hourly musters at the base to determine if anyone besides the listed flight crew was missing.

After several sweeps, it was determined that no one else was missing and the discrepancy was chalked up to a simple misunderstanding or mistaken report. I have a different take. I suspect what probably happened is that the flight officer had a manifest or Bill of Lading that listed Kosnar as being a part of the crew. However, Kosnar's retirement from flight duty probably hadn't filtered down to the flight line yet, so the flight officer probably thought he was AWOL or worse, and listed him as reporting for duty in order to cover for him. In any event, the discrepancy only added to the aura of mystery and intrigue that surrounded the disappearance.[1]

According to some reports, Taylor himself had also had bad dreams the night before the flight and when he arrived on the flight line at 1:15 PM, he requested to be relieved from flying that day. He gave no explanation. As there was no replacement instructor available, his request was denied and he subsequently disappeared along with the rest of Flight 19. So, at least two members of the flight seemed to have some sense that something would go awry that day. Believe it or not, there may be a physics connection that can account for both these incidents and the "electronic fog" that Flight 19 encountered, but we will get to that in a subsequent chapter.

Once the inquiry was completed, involved officers began to make comments to the press that only deepened the mystery. Captain W. C. Wingard, a Naval information officer told the local press "Members of the Board of Inquiry were not able to make even a good guess as to what happened." Wirshing himself said he thought that the word "disappear" should be used in reference to the case rather than "lost" as there was no proof at all that the crews were dead. Another unnamed Board member said the consensus of the investigating officers was that, "This unprecedented peacetime loss seems to be a total mystery, the strangest ever investigated in the annals of naval aviation." A Coast Guard officer and member of the Board of Inquiry was quoted as saying simply: "We don't know what the hell is going on out there," meaning the Triangle area off the Florida coast. Then things got weird. Or maybe just more honest.

A Board member who requested anonymity was quoted in the local papers as saying "They vanished as completely as if they had flown to Mars." This led to others subsequently volunteering the idea that something decidedly paranormal had occurred. J. Manson Valentine, a scientist who later worked on books about the Triangle with some of the early authors was quoted in the *Miami News* as saying:

> They are still here, but in a different dimension of a magnetic phenomenon that could have been set up by a UFO.

A mother of one of the pilots, who sat through all of the public hearings of the Board, told the press that based on what she had heard at the hearings, her conclusion was that her son was not necessarily dead, but rather "still alive somewhere in space."

Perhaps, as implied by the existence of the "secret transcript" that reporter Art Ford mentioned, the Navy knew from the beginning that something classified and paranormal had happened to Flight 19, and these quotes were their way of acknowledging to the families what had actually occurred. Certainly, the Navy never took a public stance against any of the claims that something involving the supernatural may have occurred that day.

Maybe that's because they have always known there was something "wrong" with that part of the world we now call "the Triangle."

(Endnotes)

1 *The Bermuda Triangle*, Charles Berlitz, Avon Books ISBN-13: 978-0380004652
2 Naval Air Station Fort Lauderdale Historical Association
3 McDonell, Michael (June 1973). "Lost Patrol" (PDF). Naval Aviation News: 8–16. Archived from the original (PDF) on November 2, 2004.
4 https://en.wikipedia.org/wiki/Flight_19
5 http://www.ibiblio.org/hyperwar/USN/rep/Flight19/index.html
6 https://www.nasflmuseum.com/flight-19.html
7 https://en.wikipedia.org/wiki/Flight_19

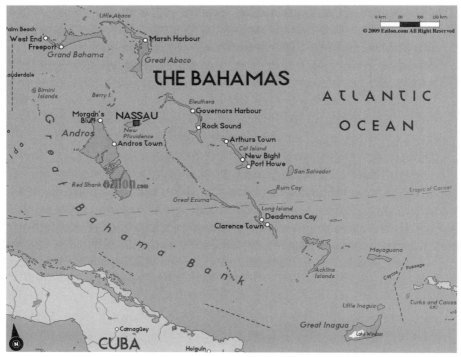

The Bahamas feature heavily in reports about the Triangle.

Chapter 3

Historical Aviation Mysteries

Following the disappearance of Flight 19 and the PBM Mariner, the number of aircraft which vanished within the boundaries of or in the vicinity of the Triangle accelerated with disturbing regularity. Although there had been plenty of major aviation mysteries and more common minor mysteries involving yachts and smaller pleasure craft prior to Flight 19, that event was really the first such incident in which a major land-sea-air search was carried out to find the missing planes. After that, major search and rescue operations involving missing or overdue aircraft became much more common if no more successful than the fruitless search for Flight 19. Aiding in the effort were advances in technology, new and better radar and communications equipment and the creation of mission specific search and rescue teams. These teams were formed with the specific purpose of not only rescuing survivors, if there were any, but also with discovering what could have possibly brought the aircraft down.

Few, if any, of these missions were successful, which only added to the mythos of the Triangle and made the government's efforts to solve the mystery of the region more intense. But after years of frustration, the government eventually abandoned the idea of explaining the mysteries and went instead to the fallback position of arguing that the number of disappearances was in no way unusual compared to any other region of the seas. The government even went to the trouble of pressuring insurance companies not to raise rates for ships or planes travelling through the area even though their own studies had indicated such measures were not only justified, but in the end cost-effective.[1]

But a closer examination of each of these cases makes it hard to argue that they are due to random events, pilot error or unpredictable weather. In fact, they seem to indicate something much stranger is going on.

On July 10, 1945, just five months before the loss of Flight 19, a US Navy PBM3S patrol seaplane, Bureau No. 6545 from the VPB2-OTU#3 Squadron was lost in the Bermuda Triangle under eerily similar circumstances. The pilot, Thomas Arthur Garner (AMM3, USN), and eleven other crew members were officially "lost at sea." The plane left the Banana River Naval Air Station in Florida at 7:07 PM on July 9, 1945 for a radar training flight to Great Exuma in the Bahamas. Their last radio position report was sent at 1:16 AM on July 10th indicating a latitude/longitude of 25-22N, 77.34W, near Providence Island, after which they were never heard from again. An extensive ten-day surface and air search, including a carrier sweep, found nothing.[2] According to a relative of one of the other crew members:

> The aircraft gave a radio transmission of 25-22N, 77-34W at 9:16 PM local time July 10th, 1945 and was not heard from after that. There was an extensive search for 21 days including a carrier sweep and then it was called off. As far as I know, nothing was ever found. According to what my Grandmother told me before she died, my uncle and Worobeck (S1c AOM Stephen WOROBECK) were good friends, having met each other in line while enlisting at Brooklyn N.Y. They went all through boot camp and AOM school in Jacksonville FL together. That's all we know.[3]

Another of the first cases that comes to mind is that of a US Army C-54 (a military version of the commercial Douglas DC-4) that took off on July 3, 1947 heading from Bermuda-Kindley Air Field NAS (NWU) toward Morrison Army Air Field in Palm Beach, Florida. At a distance of about 1,000 miles and with a maximum speed of 275 miles per hour, the plane should have arrived in Palm Beach a little over three and half hours later. It never did.

According to the few records that survive from the case, the C-54 carried a crew of six and was travelling to Palm Beach to pick up a load of cargo and supplies for American troops based in Bermuda. Shortly after takeoff, the pilot (a Major Ward, assisted by an experienced class-II navigator) reported their position as way off course, some 100 miles south of Bermuda rather than on a southwest course directly over the open sea toward Palm Beach. There was no explanation given for this logged flight plan deviation but there were rumors of a compass malfunction similar to what Flight 19 encountered a few years before.[4]

The weather was a mild 82 degrees Fahrenheit that day, and light squalls and possible mild turbulence were expected in the area but not until several hours after the aircraft had passed and, more importantly, well north of the C-54s planned route. At some point, the Bermuda tower overheard the navigator ordering a course correction which took the flight sharply north, beyond the scheduled flight path, and then again to the southwest, directly into the path of a forming squall. It is important to note that the plane was off course from the start, and these course corrections seem designed to get it back on a direct path toward Palm Beach but instead put it in the direct path of the storm, which was far north of the ideal flight path. No rational pilot/navigator would do such a thing if they had some idea where they actually were, and the fact they did this indicates that they were confused and their instrumentation was not working properly; obviously another case of the Triangle's fabled "electronic fog."

Several hours later, when the plane should have been within an hour of landing in Palm Beach, a ground radio operator heard what sounded like a faint, garbled SOS. A few minutes later, an even fainter signal was detected, followed by complete silence. The aircraft never arrived.

An immediate air-sea rescue/search was launched, with Army, Navy and Coast Guard units covering over 100,000 square miles. No wreckage was found except for some seat cushions and an air bottle about 209 miles off the coast of Florida, but they could not be directly connected to the C-54, which seemed to have vanished, once again, as if to Mars.

It's important to note that no one knows if the plane actually encountered the storm, and even if it did, the storm was quite mild. Also, no wreckage of any kind that could be directly linked to the flight was found. That didn't stop the Board of Inquiry from quickly deciding that the plane went down in a storm. According to the Aviation Safety Website:[5]

> A C-54 Skymaster was destroyed when it crashed into the Atlantic Ocean off Florida. All six on board were killed. The airplane operated on an over water flight from Bermuda-Kindley Field to West Palm Beach, FL. En route the airplane entered an area of severe weather. The pilot failed to maintain control of the airplane.
>
> Probable Cause:
>
> After considering all available facts and existing weather conditions, it is the opinion of the Accident Investigating Board at Morrison Field, Florida, that the aircraft encountered violent turbulence and the pilot lost control of the aircraft. It is possible that structural failure was a factor prior to contact with the ocean. No evidence of fire exists. There was no evidence of a ditching attempt and the debris found indicates that the crew compartment was torn apart on contact with the ocean. The last plotted position of the aircraft and the corresponding position of the frontal zone substantiates the weather assumption. Contributing factors to this accident were possible navigational error allowing aircraft to drift north of course to frontal zone and pilot error in that no apparent effort was made to circumnavigate the frontal weather.

There's only one problem with these conclusions: no evidence exists to support any of them. After looking at other cases I will present in this volume, I think it's far more likely that the C-54 encountered the Triangle's mysterious "electronic fog," the same aerial Kraken that took down Flight 19, and possibly—but not probably—was lost in the storm.

Another disturbing case is the famous *Star Tiger* disappearance we briefly covered in Chapter 1. On January 31, 1948 a British plane named *Star Tiger*, an Avro 688 Tudor Mark IV propeller

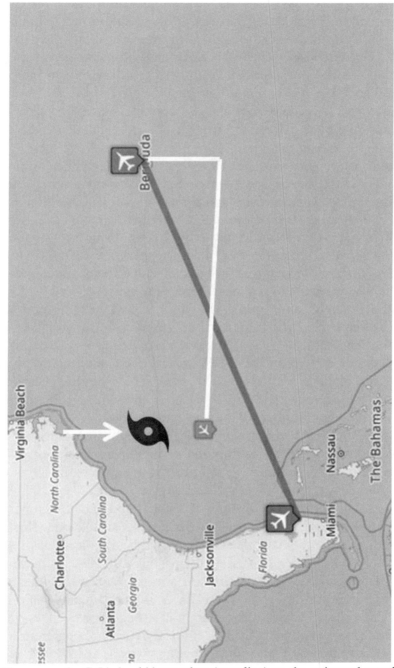

The course the C-54 should have taken (grey line) vs. the estimated actual
flight path (white) directly into a forming storm.

plane with 29 passengers aboard, simply disappeared on final approach to Bermuda after checking in several times. The plane was a well-vetted and reliable airframe, based on the British World War II Lancaster bomber. Among the passengers was Sir Arthur Coningham, a British World War II air marshal and former commander of the Second Tactical Air Force of the RAF. On a course for Bermuda from the Azores, the plane had checked in multiple times along the flight path and right up to the last transmission had reported no problems. The tower quoted the pilot's last transmission at 3:15 AM as "Weather and performance excellent. Expect to arrive on schedule." At that time, signal triangulation assumed the plane's position to be on the flight path about 380 miles from Bermuda, and it was scheduled to arrive around 5:00 AM. Nothing further was heard from the *Star Tiger*, but when the time came to check in with the tower for final instructions, no contact could be made. The tower tried again at 3:50 AM but got no response, and then again at 4:40 AM and again received no response.[6] Hoping that it was a radio problem, the tower waited for some sign of the aircraft but by 5:30 AM it was apparent the plane was overdue. The tower declared an emergency and a massive search operation commenced involving at least 26 planes and 10 Coast Guard and Navy ships. The search lasted for five days and 882 flight hours but all they found were a few barrels and boxes that were hundreds of miles off the last known flight path of the *Star Tiger*. They appeared to have been dumped overboard by a ship rather than be part of a plane crash, and there was no oil slick or any other wreckage nearby. Over the next few days, things got even stranger.

As with the mystery of Flight 19, ham radio operators reported on some strange occurrences in the days that followed. Several listeners along the Atlantic coast reported hearing a series of dots similar to Morse code. The garbled signal spelled out a single word: "Tiger," and was overheard and reported by at *least two* hams at around the same time. Then, a Coast Guard station in Newfoundland Canada reported that it had received a voice message clearly speaking the letters G-A-H-N-P, the exact call letters of the *Star Tiger*. Once again, it was as if someone were sending ghostly messages from beyond this plane of existence.

Because the flight contained a member of the British knighthood, once the search was called off an immediate Court of Inquiry was formed headed by Lord Hugh Macmillan. The investigation, which was held in public at Church House, Westminster, opened on April 12, 1948 and lasted 11 days. On August 21 it presented its report to Lord Pakenham, who had succeeded Lord Nathan of Churt as Minister of Civil Aviation. The report emphasized that the crew of the *Star Tiger* were highly experienced, and found "want of care and attention to detail" in the flight plan, but nothing serious enough to explain the disappearance. The plane had plenty of fuel, and, despite a maintenance issue on one of the engines before it left its initial port of Lisbon, could have flown on with three or even two of the four engines it carried. The report went through all the available information and gave the following timeline:

On the morning of January 28, 1948, the crew and passengers boarded *Star Tiger* at Lisbon only to be forced to return to the airport waiting room when the pilot, Captain Brian W. McMillan, told them that the port inner engine needed some attention. The aircraft took off 2-1/2 hours later, and made what was intended to be a 75-minute refueling stop at Santa Maria in the Azores. However, the reported weather was so poor that Captain McMillan decided they should stop over until the next day.

The following day *Star Tiger* took off for the next leg of its flight to Bermuda despite strong winds. McMillan had decided to fly at no more than 2,000 feet so as to avoid the worst winds. An Avro Lancastrian belonging to British South American Airways (BSAA) piloted by Frank Griffin took off an hour ahead of the *Star Tiger*, and Griffin had agreed to radio weather information back to *Star Tiger*.

Star Tiger took off at 15:34 and soon after takeoff was lashed by heavy rain and strong winds. At first some 200 miles behind the Lancastrian, McMillan slowly closed the distance between them and the aircraft remained in radio contact with each other and with Bermuda. The second pilot aboard the *Star Tiger* was David Colby DFC, like McMillan a highly experienced pilot and ex-RAF Pathfinder Force squadron leader.

By 1:26 AM on January 30th, after 10 hours in the air, *Star Tiger* was only 150 miles behind the Lancastrian. The navigator of the Lancastrian managed to fix their position using celestial navigation and found that the winds had blown the aircraft 60 miles off track in the previous hour. By this time, *Star Tiger* had passed its Point of No Alternative, at which it could have diverted to Newfoundland, and was committed to remaining on course for Bermuda.

At about 2:00 AM, Cyril Ellison, *Star Tiger*'s navigator, fixed the aircraft's position and learned that they too had been blown off course and were crabbing away from Bermuda. He gave McMillan a new course which turned the aircraft directly into a gale. However, McMillan still expected to reach Bermuda with at least an hour's worth of fuel remaining upon landing.

At 03:00 Captain Griffin aboard the Lancastrian amended his ETA from 3:56 to 5:00 AM, and called *Star Tiger* to say that he was switching to voice telephony to contact Bermuda Approach Control. Griffin later testified that he heard nothing from *Star Tiger* to indicate that it was in trouble, and that from then until he touched down at 4:11 AM his own aircraft encountered no turbulence, icing, fog or electrical storms.

At 3:04 AM Radio Officer Robert Tuck aboard *Star Tiger* requested a radio bearing from Bermuda, but the signal was not strong enough to obtain an accurate reading. Tuck repeated the request 11 minutes later, and this time the Bermuda radio operator was able to obtain a bearing of 72 degrees, accurate to within 2 degrees. The Bermuda operator transmitted this information, and Tuck acknowledged receipt at 3:17 AM. This was the last communication with the aircraft. The Bermuda operator tried to contact *Star Tiger* at 3:50 AM and, receiving no reply, thought that it had gone over to direct radio contact with Bermuda Approach Control. However, Approach Control reported this was not the case. The Bermuda radio operator tried at 04:05 to contact *Star Tiger*, again without success, and after trying again at 4:40 AM he declared a state of emergency. He had heard no distress message, and neither had anyone else, even though many receiving stations were listening on *Star Tiger*'s frequency.[7]

All of this led to the Court declaring:

In closing this report it may truly be said that no more

baffling problem has ever been presented for investigation. In the complete absence of any reliable evidence as to either the nature or the cause of the accident of *Star Tiger* the Court has not been able to do more than suggest possibilities, none of which reaches the level even of probability. Into all activities which involve the co-operation of man and machine two elements enter of a very diverse character.

There is an incalculable element of the human equation dependent upon imperfectly known factors; and there is the mechanical element subject to quite different laws. A breakdown may occur in either separately or in both in conjunction. Or some external cause may overwhelm both man and machine. What happened in this case will never be known and the fate of *Star Tiger* must remain an unsolved mystery.

In other words, we have no clue what happened to the plane. Not even a hint. Just like Flight 19.

Then, things started to get *really* weird. A year later, once again in the Triangle, the *Star Tiger's* sister ship, *Star Ariel*, also disappeared in the Bermuda Triangle. On January 17, 1949, just 12 days before the first anniversary of the vanishing of the *Star Tiger*, the *Star Ariel* left Bermuda carrying a crew of 7 and 13 passengers. The final destination was Kingston, Jamaica. The *Star Ariel* was actually not expected to fly that day but when another BSAA Tudor IV named *Star Lion* lost an engine on approach to Bermuda, the *Star Ariel* was pressed into service as a replacement for the final leg of the journey.

When the *Star Ariel* took off at 08:41 she was piloted by Captain John Clutha McPhee, 34, a veteran pilot with the Royal New Zealand Air Force. Weather conditions were fair and McPhee received clearance to take a high altitude course because of the high ceiling. After takeoff, he quickly guided the *Star Ariel* to 18,000 feet altitude in anticipation of a smooth flight. About an hour into the flight McPhee contacted Kingston by radio:

> I departed from Kindley Field at 8:41 a.m. hours. My ETA at Kingston 2:10 p.m. hours. I am flying in good

visibility at 18,000 feet. I flew over 150 miles south of Kindley Field at 9:32 hours. My ETA at 30° N is 9:37 hours. Will you accept control?

And then at 09:42:

I was over 30° N at 9:37 I am changing frequency to MRX.[8]

Another version of what was essentially the same dialog between McPhee and the control tower was published by Charles Berlitz in his book *The Bermuda Triangle*:

This is Captain McPhee aboard the *Ariel* en route to Kingston, Jamaica, from Bermuda. We have reached cruising altitude. Fair weather. Expected time of arrival Kingston as scheduled. I am changing radio frequency to pick up Kingston.

Whichever version is correct, nothing further was ever heard from the *Star Ariel* or her pilot, at least not officially. It was reported that MacDill Field air base in Florida picked up a transmission from a ship named the *Santa Inez* out of Puerto Rico to the effect that it had received faint "distress signals" over a period of two hours, but this was never confirmed, and in any event it seems impossible that a plane could be in distress for two hours without going down. It was almost as if *Star Ariel* was caught in another of the mysterious time altering fogs the Triangle was becoming so famous for.

An immediate message was sent all over the area off the Florida coast calling for a search:

British South American Airways four-engined air-aircraft Star Ariel/Gagre which departed Bermuda 1242 GMT 17th January for Jamaica on track two one six degrees was last heard from when approximately 15 miles south of Bermuda at 1337 GMT 17th Jan. All vessels are requested to report to this station the sighting of any floating debris in the nature of aircraft cabin upholstery and pillows; colour blue, aircraft dinghies colour yellow, Mae Wests colour dark brown, all of which would be marked BSAA, or any floating clothing.

The search for the *Star Ariel* was immediately commenced with a large force that included another Tudor IV, the G-AHNJ *Star Panther*. She had earlier landed at Nassau, and after refueling took off at 15:25 to fly out to *Star Ariel*'s route, bisect it, and follow it back to Bermuda. Another aircraft took off from Bermuda, flew 500 miles, then did a 10 mile lattice search all the way back. A US Navy task force headed by the battleship USS *Missouri* and including the aircraft carriers USS *Kearsarge* and USS *Leyte* assisted in the search, which expanded to dozens of ships and several planes over the next few days.[6]

By January 19 the search had been broadened to an area of 55,000 square miles southwest of Bermuda. United States Air Force Major Keith Cloe, who had been put in charge of the operation, said that the search would be continued until January 22nd and extended if any reports of debris were received.[9] The search was finally abandoned on January 23rd, with aircraft from Kindley Field having flown over 1,000,000 miles. No sign of debris, oil slicks or wreckage had been found, although according to Berlitz, there were reports of a "strange light" in the sea from both a British and American search plane. The Air Force sent a search and rescue team to the area, but again, nothing was found.

A Board of Enquiry, the Brabazon Committee, was formed to investigate the disappearance of the *Star Ariel* as well as review the disappearance of the *Star Tiger* one year earlier. Among other things, it found no obvious design flaw or problem with the Tudor IV airplane itself, and noted that while other aircraft of the type had crashed due to pilot error, the two sister aircraft were the only ones that had ever simply disappeared altogether.

On December 21, 1949 the report was issued by the Chief Inspector of Accidents, Air Commodore Vernon Brown, CB, OBE, MA, FRAeS.[10] In it, he stated that, "through lack of evidence due to no wreckage having been found, the cause of the accident is unknown."

Brown said that there was no evidence of defect in, or failure of, any part of the aircraft before its departure from Bermuda. The takeoff weight and the center of gravity were within the prescribed limits; a daily inspection had been carried out; the pilot was experienced on the route; the radio officer was very experienced and also experienced on the route; good radio communications had been maintained with the aircraft up to and including reception of its last message; there were no weather complications, and a study of the weather reports gave no reason to believe that the accident was caused by meteorological conditions. There was also no evidence of sabotage, though Brown said that the possibility of such could not be entirely eliminated.

It was accepted that radio communications were poor during the early afternoon and worsened between 16:00 and 17:00, but Brown said it seemed strange that no attempt was made by BSAA staff at Kingston to find out whether anything had been heard of the aircraft until 2 hours 28 minutes after its last radio transmission. Kingston also did not attempt to establish contact with the aircraft until 17:10 or inquire as to whether it had made contact with Nassau or New York or any other radio station.[5]

The bottom line is that no plausible cause for either aircraft's loss could be found, since both vanished, apparently in midair, without a trace. The most bizarre aspect of the two mysteries is the reports of the time-delayed transmissions from both aircraft, as if both had disappeared into some kind of electronic time warp from which a few faint electromagnetic signals had escaped. It is easy to see why these two cases were so important to the mystery and lore of the Triangle.

But there is another reason the disappearance of the *Star Ariel* caused so much consternation about the Triangle. Less than a week before the loss of the *Star Ariel*, another similar passenger aircraft had also disappeared into the Triangle without a trace. A Douglas DST airliner, registered NC16002, disappeared near the end of a trip from Puerto Rico to Miami on December 28, 1948.

Captained by pilot Robert Linquist, assisted by co-pilot Ernest Hill and stewardess Mary Burke, the aircraft ended its Miami-San Juan leg at 7:40 Eastern Standard Time on December 27. Linquist informed local repair crewmen that a landing gear warning light was not functioning and that the aircraft batteries were discharged and low on water. Unwilling to delay the aircraft's scheduled takeoff for Miami for several hours, Linquist said the batteries would be recharged by the aircraft's generators en route.[11]

Linquist taxied NC16002 to the end of runway 27 for takeoff, but stopped at the end of the apron due to lack of two-way radio communication. Although capable of receiving, Linquist reported to the head of Puerto Rican Transport—who had driven out to the aircraft—that the radio could not transmit because of the low batteries. After agreeing to stay close to San Juan until they were recharged enough to allow two-way contact, NC16002 finally lifted off at 10:03 PM Eastern Standard Time. After circling the city for 11 minutes, Linquist received confirmation from CAA at San Juan and told the tower that they were proceeding to Miami on the previous flight plan. Apparently the radio transmission problem had been fixed.

The weather was fair with high visibility, but the aircraft did not respond to subsequent calls from San Juan. At 10:23, the Overseas Foreign Air Route Traffic Control Center at Miami heard a routine transmission from NC16002, wherein Linquist reported they were at 8,300 feet and had an ETA in Miami of 4:03AM. His message placed the flight about 700 miles from Miami at the time, meaning that regardless of the radio problems the plane was more than halfway toward its destination. Transmissions were heard sporadically throughout the night by Miami, but all were routine.

At 4:13AM, Linquist reported he was 50 miles south of Miami:

> We are approaching the field... Only fifty miles out to the south... We can see the lights of Miami now. All's well. Will stand by for landing instructions.

The transmission was not heard at Miami but was monitored at New Orleans, Louisiana, some 600 miles away, and was relayed to Miami. The accident investigation report issued by the Civil Aeronautics Board said the pilot may have incorrectly reported his position, but no proof of this claim exists, it is just speculation by the Board.[12]

Miami weather was reported clear but the wind had moved

from the northwest to northeast. The accident investigation report said Miami transmitted the wind change information but neither Miami nor New Orleans was able to contact the flight so it is unknown whether NC16002 received it. Without this knowledge the aircraft could have drifted 40 to 50 miles off course, which widened the search area to include hills in Cuba, the Everglades and even Gulf of Mexico waters.

On January 4, 1949, two bodies were found 50 miles south of Guantanamo Bay, Cuba but it could not be established that they were passengers or crew connected to the missing flight.[13] Nothing further was heard from Linquist and the aircraft was never found. A plane similar to the DC-3 has been found by divers in the Bermuda Triangle, but it has yet to be connected to the missing plane.

Besides the massive search, a full investigation of the disappearance was initiated and reached the following findings of fact:

- The aircraft was originally built on 12 June 1936, and had a total of 28,257 flying hours prior to the landing in San Juan. It had been inspected several times in the previous two years and certified to be airworthy.

- The aircraft was given a partial overhaul, including the replacement of both engines, in November 1948. An in-flight test was conducted to judge the results of the overhaul, including flying to New Jersey and back. Again, the aircraft was certified to be airworthy.

- Although the carrier, aircraft, and crew were certified, at the time of takeoff, the aircraft did not meet the requirements of the operating certificate. How it differed was not specified.

- The company's maintenance records were sloppy and incomplete. In one case, a subcontractor working on an engine in October 1948 completed the task but did not save any records proving it.

- Captain Linquist told San Juan that his landing gear down indicator lamps did not work. This led to the discovery that his batteries were low on water and electrical charge. While he ordered the refilling of the batteries with water, he ordered the reinstallation of the batteries on board the aircraft without recharging them.

• The aircraft left with the batteries charged only enough to satisfy two-way radio communication with the tower, with the understanding that an in-flight flight plan would be filed before they left the vicinity of San Juan. This was not done, and the plane continued on a course for Miami. It was noted in the report that the plane's radio transmitter did not function properly due to the low battery charge.

• The aircraft left San Juan with a cargo/passenger weight 118 pounds over the allowable limit.

• A message was sent to the plane concerning a change in wind direction that could have been strong enough to push the plane off course. It was not known if the plane received the message.

• The plane's electrical system was not functioning normally prior to departing San Juan.

• The aircraft had fuel for 7-1/2 hours of flight; at the time the last transmission was intercepted, the flight had gone on for 6 hours and 10 minutes after takeoff, and thus "an error in location would be critical."

• Because of a lack of wreckage and other information, probable cause for the loss of the aircraft could not be determined.

Separately, none of these mechanical flaws or human errors could have resulted in the loss of the air vehicle. But any number of them combined might have ultimately contributed to its demise. Still, while there were some risks taken by the pilot, the weather was generally fair and no credible scenario to explain the loss has ever been put forth. For the moment at least, the case of the missing DC-3 remains a likely subject of the Triangle's hunger for mystery.

These disappearances, at least in the early days of the Triangle mystery, seemed to happen in clusters and follow the same pattern. There were nine further small plane disappearances that took place in December 1949 and January 1950 alone, all following the same pattern of normal takeoff in good weather, followed by routine radio transmissions and then at some point along the route, the complete disappearance of the airplane, passengers and crew. No wreckage, bodies or even an oil slick were ever found.

The unexplainable disappearances continued into the 1950s and 60s. Like the wave of incidents in the late 1940s, these once again followed a pattern of generally occurring in the December to March wintertime period. Berlitz referred to a number of these in his book.

In March 1951, a US Globemaster C-124 disappeared on the northern end of the Triangle while on its way to Ireland. The Globemaster radioed in that while still within the boundaries of the Triangle as it is sometimes defined, it was being forced to ditch in the late afternoon of March 23, 1951. Somehow, there had been an explosion in the cargo bay and the ensuing fire forced the pilots to ditch the aircraft in the Atlantic Ocean several hundred nautical miles west-southwest of Ireland. According to the logbook of the USCG Cutter *Casco*, the ditching and subsequent evacuation were

A C-124 Globemaster.

successful, but when *Casco* arrived at the ditching position, the aircraft and its occupants had completely vanished.

The aircraft landed safely and intact and all hands then donned life preservers and climbed into inflatable five-man rafts equipped with numerous survival supplies, including food, water, signal flares, cold-weather gear, and "Gibson Girl" hand crank emergency radios. Bizarrely, the crew and the plane were spotted by a Boeing B-50 Superfortress from the 509th Bomb Wing Detachment which was en route from RAF base Lakenheath in Suffolk, England. The Superfortress pilots reported spotting the survivors in rafts and seeing flares. The aircraft carrier USS *Coral Sea* was dispatched to conduct rescue operations but when it arrived 19 hours later, the plane and the crew had completely disappeared in calm seas with no wind. Nothing was ever found.

On February 2, 1952, a British York transport carrying 33 passengers and six crew members simply vanished on the northern edge of the Triangle while on its way to Jamaica.[14] Some weak SOS signals were received but were almost immediately cut off. Prior to that, the Avro York aircraft had reported in at regular one-hour intervals from the time it left its refueling stop in the Azores. They reported nothing unusual. A public inquiry was opened in London at Holborn Town Hall on July 2, 1953 to consider possible causes of the loss of the plane. The Solicitor General representing the Crown absolved the crew from blame and also ruled out sabotage or contaminated fuel as possible explanations.

On the second day, the Chief Investigation Officer of the Accidents Investigation Branch (AIB) gave an opinion that it may have been an uncontrollable fire in one of the aircraft's engines, but could offer no evidence to support his thesis. The final report of the inquiry was issued on December 3, 1953 and stated that the cause was "unascertainable." The court found the loss could not be attributed to any "wrongful act or default of any person or party." It was concluded that the SOS signal was transmitted at a normal urgency and was not necessarily an indication that urgent assistance was required. This was quickly followed by a hasty distress signal that indicated that whatever trouble had developed, it happened in a sudden and violent manner. In the end, it was just another plane swallowed up by the enigma of the Bermuda

Triangle without a trace.

Less than two years later on October 30, 1954, a US Navy Super Constellation R7V-1 aircraft disappeared while flying in fair weather from Patuxent River Naval Air Station, Maryland, to Lajes in the Azores. According to records from the time, there were 42 passengers and crew members aboard. Designated Flight 441, most of the passengers were US Naval officers and their families who were being transferred to overseas destinations. The pilot was an experienced officer named Lt. Leonard. After an uneventful takeoff at 9:39 PM in fair weather, the aircraft headed basically due east toward the Azores. Because of the fair weather, Leonard promptly flew the plane to about 17,000 feet, which should have led to a smooth and equally uneventful flight. Flight 441 then radioed back its position in regular intervals, with the last transmission being heard from the plane at 11:30 PM when Flight 441 was between 350 and 400 miles off the east coast of the United States. It was never heard from again.[15]

According to Berlitz, more than 200 planes and multiple surface vessels joined in searching several hundred square miles of ocean in the area of the last transmission but found nothing. Like many of the other cases a faint SOS was supposedly heard less than an hour after the plane's last radio contact, but this was never confirmed. Like so many other disappearances in the Triangle, it ended up being attributed to a phantom signal, perhaps from deep within the mouth of the electronic cloud which had claimed it.

A board of inquiry was once again launched and as in the previous cases, no fault or cause could be ascertained, although it did conclude that a light weather system had moved into the plane's flight path sometime after takeoff:

> Lt. Leonard has been flying the North Atlantic routes for the past two years and it is thought that he was very familiar with this kind of weather.

The final report stated:

> His choice of 17,000 feet altitude for this flight was a good one. According to the weather cross-section, 19,000

feet would have been an even better altitude. At any rate he should have been on top (of any weather systems), for the most part, except for (an) occasional buildup. It must be pointed out that the R7V-1 was equipped with ASP-42 Airborne Radar and is always used when flying this sort of weather.

The Board also reported that, "The possibility of structural failure during transit of frontal weather cannot be discounted in this accident, but the possibility appears remote." Of Lt. Leonard's capabilities as a pilot, the Board concluded:

> Lt. Leonard was well trained in thunderstorm penetration speed and technique. It is thought that if he did enter a thunderstorm he would have entered at the correct speed and would have flown the up and down drafts without fighting them. The weather that Lt. Leonard was thought to have been subjected to was not beyond the capabilities of R7V-1, nor was it thought to be beyond his own capabilities.

Keep in mind that there is no evidence whatsoever that Flight 441 encountered a thunderstorm. The tower did not warn him of one and he never indicated any weather was encountered at any point before the plane disappeared. Also, the plane's cargo manifest listed 111 life vests, 46 exposure suits, 660 paper cups and 5 life rafts aboard the aircraft. Since all of these items float in water and none of these were ever found, it seems unlikely that the plane actually crashed or ditched at sea. It simply disappeared in midair.

In the end, the board asserted—with no evidence—that the plane had encountered some undefinable "violent force" in midair, although it could offer no suggestion as to what that might have been. "It is the opinion of the Board that R7V-1, BuNo 128441 did meet with a sudden and violent force, that rendered the aircraft no longer airworthy, and was thereby beyond the scope of human endeavor to control. The force that rendered the aircraft uncontrollable is *unknown*."

Or simply unrecognizable and supernatural…

After a fairly quiet 1955, things picked up again in the Triangle in the spring of 1956. Berlitz cites the case a Boeing B-25 bomber which had been converted to a cargo-carrying civilian plane which disappeared over the Tongue of the Ocean on April 5, 1956. I can find no other sources for this alleged incident and have not been able to verify it. However, on November 9, 1956, a US Navy Martin Marlin P5M patrol seaplane vanished at sea while on patrol with a crew of 10. No other information seems to be readily available on that case.

There were no further prominent disappearances after that until 1961, when an entire B-52 Stratofortress simply disappeared while on a training exercise near Bermuda.[16] The case is little known but it is extraordinary.

According to blogger and author "Gian J. Quasar" (obviously a pen name) "Pogo 22" was the code name given to a B-52 Stratofortress bomber involved in an exercise named "Sky Shield II" which took place on October 14, 1961. The purpose of the Sky Shield exercises (there were four planned) was for nuclear strike deterrent bomber preparedness. Six B-52s were to partake, all from Seymour Johnson AFB in North Carolina.

The Sky Shield II operation was actually the second exercise under the broader program conducted in the Atlantic. The first Sky Shield was a success with seven of eight British Vulcan aircraft completing their nuclear bombing practice runs and returning to base safely. There were some problems with civilian interference, so planning for Sky Shield II was more organized and thorough than the first operation. In August 1961, the Aircraft Owners and Pilots Association published an article in its *Pilot Magazine* saying, "Don't Forget Sky Shield," and reminded pilots about the upcoming exercise. "If you've planned a flight for Oct. 14 or 15, better look at the clock before you take off." An estimated 2,900 US and Canadian flights, scheduled to carry around 125,000 passengers, were cancelled for those days.

Operation Sky Shield II commenced on October 14, 1961 with exercises planned from 11:00 AM to 11:00 PM that day. It was one of the largest defense exercises ever held in the Western Hemisphere and involved on the order of 250 bombers against

250 missile sites and some 1,800 fighter planes flying more than 6,000 sorties. More than 50 US fighter-interceptor squadrons also participated, including those equipped with McDonnell F-101B Voodoos, Convair F-106 Delta Darts and F-102 Delta Daggers, Lockheed F-104 Starfighters, Northrop F-89J Scorpions, and Douglas F4D Skyrays.[17] Across the North American continent some 150,000 airfield and flying personnel and 50,000 more in close support also played a part, spanning NORAD, the US Air Force, Army, Navy, Air National Guard, and the Royal Canadian Air Force.[18] During Sky Shield II, the RAF Vulcans participated again with four from the 27th Squadron (serials XJ824, XH555, XJ823, and one other), again flying from Kindley Air Force Base, Bermuda, and four aircraft from the 83rd Squadron flying from RAF Lossiemouth, in Scotland. They simulated Russian heavy bombers operating at 56,000 feet above the United States Air Force B-52 Stratofortresses, which were flying at 35-42,000 feet. Below them, B-47 Stratojets were also part of the formation. One 27th Squadron Vulcan, flying from Bermuda, successfully evaded the defending F-102 Delta Dagger interceptors and, covered by the other three jamming operations, tracked round to the north and landed at Plattsburgh Air Force Base, New York. The northern force attacking in a stream reported a single instance of radar contact by an interceptor and all four landed in Newfoundland.

General Laurence Kuter was quoted in various media sources after Sky Shield II. In comments appearing in periodicals ranging from *Air Force Magazine* to the *Chicago Tribune*, he called Sky Shield II "the greatest exercise in information analysis, decision-making, and action-taking in continental aerospace defense in all our history." But Kuter deflected calls for a score of the operation, reiterating that Sky Shield's intent was, "by no means, a contest between offensive and defensive forces."

After the operation, NORAD produced an exhaustive report, presented it to the Joint Chiefs of Staff, and then filed it in secure archives. It wasn't until 1997 that most, but not all, of the Sky Shield results were declassified. Conclusions showed that nearly one-half of enemy flights at low altitude had escaped detection, and of those initially detected, 40 percent then eluded tracking radar by changing their formation shape, size, or altitude. No more than one-fourth of bombers in Sky Shield II would have been intercepted. What they did not cover in any detail was the loss of one of the B-52s.

Wikipedia's page on the operation reported the disappearance of the B-52 with a single, simple paragraph which contained no details drawn from public records:

> A B-52 lost in the Atlantic Ocean accounted for the 8 lives lost during the exercise. On 15 October 1961, a search triangle 600 miles from New York was set up looking for the missing crew. A US Coast Guard (USCG) cutter reported seeing an orange flare at 12:15 a.m. on the 17 of October, but the eight crew members were eventually presumed lost at sea. These were the only casualties of the three (Sky Shield) operations.

There was, however, a bit more to it.

Most of the details we now know about the loss of the "Pogo 22" aircraft were tracked down by Quasar. He wrote:

> It was merely by accident that I discovered it through a book by Coast Guard Capt. John Waters (*Rescue at Sea*), in which he talked about Coast Guard search operations. In passing he mentioned a B-52 vanished, yet without even mentioning what ocean. The Air Force Safety Center found the report in their vaults. It is from this that the following was gleaned.[14]

According to Quasar, there were six B-52s scheduled to participate in Sky Shield II, broken into three groups of two each. Their destination was a waypoint in the North Atlantic off Newfoundland where they would rendezvous and in-flight refuel with three KC-135 Stratotankers. They would then fly on to their designated targets and commence their attack runs. The purpose was to simulate in time, distance and difficulty a possible attack run on Soviet Russian targets. The six crews were given the normal operational briefing between 9 and 9:30 AM by Captain Howard Whitehurst, the 4241st's Weather Officer and were told to expect "no significant weather" along the flight path. The planes were given code call signs for the exercise and "Pogo 22" was the designation for the B-52 commanded by Captain Roland C. Starke Jr. Pogo 22 was designated the "White Cell" leader, and was to take off in tandem with Pogo 13 at "H" hour, 1700 Zulu—i.e., 12 PM. They both took off with 215,000 pounds of fuel and made a controlled climb south of Norfolk, Virginia. They were to maintain radio silence until within 100 miles of their refueling waypoint off Newfoundland.

When this time came, about three hours after takeoff, Pogo 22 pilot Lieutenant Ken Payne reported that they could not pick up the KC-135's beacon and home in on it. The KC-135 replied likewise that the B-52 simply did not show up either. This sounds suspiciously like the Bermuda Triangle's "electronic fog" rearing its ugly head again, but Lieutenant Payne brushed it aside and decided he would make the rendezvous visually. Right on target, Pogos 13 and 22 rendezvoused with the KC-135 at 3 PM. Afterward they both turned south toward Bermuda to continue the second leg of the mission.

According to Quasar, inter-plane dialogue was then picked up indicating a disagreement over course. Pogo 13 was sure they weren't following the planned flight track back. Payne and Starke checked with Dean Upp, the head navigator and they mutually agreed to change course to Pogo 13's estimate. Again, this smacks of the mysterious instrument problems that so many flights had encountered in the Triangle.

They were now roughly 500 miles northeast of Bermuda, with a flight track that would swoop them down in a large inverted arc north of the island and from there they would fly back to North Carolina and home.

For the next hour they kept each other in sight. Aside from the snag in not being able to detect the KC-135 beacon all had gone off very well.

At 4:15 PM, Pogo 13 and Pogo 22 were in sight of each other, except for "short intervals when passing through cloud layers" while descending to a lower altitude. At about 300 miles northeast (near where *Star Tiger* vanished) of Bermuda all the cells split up according to orders. They separated to 10 miles distance, in lateral positions to each other, and raced toward the coast. Pogo 22 was the northern most.

They dropped to 1,000 feet elevation, according to orders. When the formation was about three miles apart Pogo 13 caught her last glimpse of Pogo 22. Everything was apparently normal and visibility was 7 to 10 miles. There was no reason to think that anything could now overtake a huge eight-engine aircraft.

But something evidently went terribly wrong.

Pogo 22 was never seen again. It seems certain there was no midair explosion. At only 10 miles distant they were still in visual range, and that kind of explosion and trail of smoke would have been noticed. Pogo 22 had simply vanished. Silently. And suddenly.

Once it was discovered that Pogo 22 did not land with the other craft, a massive search was initiated. Although over 280,000 square miles of seas were searched, as often was the case, no trace of the aircraft was ever found. Given that this was a military aircraft possibly carrying nuclear weapons and on a classified training mission, it's safe to assume no expense was spared in the search. Yet, like so many other such incidents in the history of the Triangle, it was fruitless. It seems that Pogo 22 was simply snatched out of thin air. But by who? Or what?

The odd disappearances continued into the next year. In 1962, a US Air Force KB-50 tanker from Langley AFB in Langley, Virginia disappeared on its way to Lajes in the Azores under circumstances eerily similar to the Super Constellation Flight 441 eight years before. According to sources,[19] the flight, designated "Tyler 41" and piloted by Major Bob Tawney, left in broad daylight at 11:17 AM on January the 8th and sent routine messages every hour. Tawney indicated he was flying at 385 miles per hour at 23,000 feet in fair weather on an easterly heading towards the Azores. At 1 PM Tawney, or his copilot Zoltan Szaloki, were overheard by a Navy transport plane about an hour behind them. They were trying to raise the Ernest Harmon Air Force Base control tower, then other stations along the east coast. Between 1:10 and 1:20 PM, Tawney was able to contact the Navy transport and informed the crew of his position, asking them to relay it back.

However, the transport was also having radio difficulties. So with little else to do, Tawney finally just signed off and continued toward the Azores. They were just north of Bermuda at this point, near where Pogo 22 had vanished just months before, and the *Star Tiger* had 14 years earlier. By 7 PM Tyler 41 was overdue and the Lajes tower was becoming nervous. When an immediate radio search failed to reach them, a huge search was ordered and began at 8:15 PM.

According to the Bermuda Triangle Database,[14] the Commander, United States Forces, Azores (COMUSFORAZ), launched a huge search involving 162 sorties flown for over 1,369 hours by the US Air Force alone, with an additional 7 sorties and 49 search hours by the US Navy, and 23 sorties in 236 hours by the US Coast Guard. In addition, there were 5 Coast Guard cutters which searched the entire flight track of the KB-50 from Langley to the Azores, a 412 hour search covering 440,820 square miles of the Atlantic, to date the largest search for any lost plane or ship. There was an oil slick cited in the loose vicinity of Tyler 41's flight path, but it could not be specifically traced to the flight and Tawney's last known position was well away from it. The final results of the massive search were summed up in the narrative of the accident report. "No trace of any survivors or wreckage was ever found, thus preventing the accident Board from obtaining any physical evidence upon which to base their investigation." It simply disappeared.

One of the prevalent trends in all these cases is that of "fog" or "electronic fog" reports associated with the disappearances. There seems to be something about the area of the Triangle that gives rise to this strange effect that simply does not happen anywhere else on the planet and which does not seem to be associated with any known weather phenomenon. Even if it was, there is no known weather phenomenon which causes disruption of radio signals to the point that they seem to cause a time delay effect as we see in the Triangle cases.

Berlitz goes on to list even more cases from the 1960s. He cites the case of an SOS from a private plane flying to Nassau in the Bahamas in the vicinity of Great Abaco Island. Although he does not give an exact date for this incident, according to him the morning weather was excellent, but the pilot soon found himself flying through fog and was unable to give his position or even see the islands below him, in spite of clear visibility apparent to other observers in the surrounding area. It was as if the fog had surrounded just his plane, creating confusion and possibly leading to an accident. Berlitz noted that "In this case the plane did not completely vanish, as a part of one wing was later found floating in the sea." This implies that perhaps the fog is a multidimensional effect, like a time warp of some kind, which can either envelop a plane completely or cause sufficient confusion for a genuine accident to occur back in the "real" world.

Another example of this was an August 28, 1963 case of two KC-135 Stratotankers. The tankers had left Homestead Air Force Base in Florida on a mission to conduct a midair refueling of a pair of B-47 bombers on a training mission. They disappeared after completing their mission and reporting their position as some 300 mile west of Bermuda. An intensive search located probable debris from one of the lost planes about 260 miles southwest of Bermuda, and investigators concluded that there had been a collision between the two planes.

Several days later, however, more debris, thought to come from the other plane, was found 160 miles away. If they had collided in the air, despite an official Air Force statement that they were not flying close together, then something must have separated the wreckage much more quickly than the ocean currents could have done. The simple fact is it is not possible to have two debris fields so far apart if a midair collision occurred. And, if they had both crashed simultaneously, but not into each other—perhaps as the five Avengers had—what would have caused their instruments or engines to malfunction at the same time? As Berlitz notes, the official explanation for this one is very thin indeed.

More disappearances followed. On September 22, 1963 a C-133 Cargomaster disappeared between Delaware and its destination in the Azores. The last message from the pilot indicated that all was well as he gave his position at about 80 miles off the south Jersey coast. An intensive search by planes, Coast Guard and Navy vessels continued until September 25, but found nothing that could be identified with the missing plane. Nevertheless, the official narrative was "Crashed at sea, en route from Dover AFB

A C-133 Cargomaster.

to Lajes AFB, Azores. The plane was last heard from 57 minutes after it took off." How could they know it had "crashed at sea" when not a trace of the plane was found?

On June 5, 1965, a C-119 "Flying Boxcar" on a routine mission and carrying a crew of ten vanished while on a flight from Homestead Air Force Base to Grand Turk Island, near the Bahamas. The Flying Boxcar had arrived at Homestead AFB at 5:04 PM and was prepared for a flight to Grand Turk Island in Turks and Caicos. It then took off at 7:47 PM with four additional mechanics who were to fix the engine of a sister C-119 stranded on Grand Turk. The airplane never arrived at the destination and was declared missing. The last radio call came from just north of Crooked Island, 177 miles from Grand Turk Island.[20]

The coast guard conducted an extensive five-day search, covering about 77,000 square miles per day. Nothing was found. The Coast Guard eventually simply reported "Results negative" and "There are no conjectures," as to what happened to the plane. On July 18, 1965 debris from the missing plane was found on a beach of Gold Rock Cay just off the northeast shore of Acklins Island. Berlitz says that there was a faint but unintelligible message heard which faded away "as if something were blocking radio transmission, or else that the plane was receding, as has been suggested, farther and farther into space and time." Another plane flying in the same flight path but in the opposite direction reported fair weather and excellent visibility. Again, what could

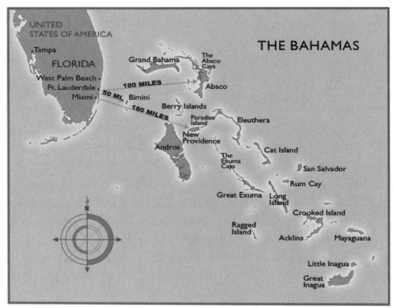

have happened to the plane?

Perhaps a clue emerged in the June 7, 1964 case of Carolyn Cascio, a licensed pilot who disappeared with a friend while en route from Nassau to Grand Turk Island in the Bahamas. According to Berlitz, when Cascio arrived at the location where Grand Turk should be, she reported that she was unable to ascertain her heading and was circling two "unidentified islands" which she was sure were not Grand Turk because "Nothing is down there." No sign of civilization, an airport, nothing. Getting more desperate, she radioed down asking "Is there any way out of this?" and seemed confused.

Observers on Grand Turk island reported that at the same time of day they saw a light plane matching her aircraft's description circling the island for over 30 minutes before vanishing. If this was Cascio's plane, why didn't she land? And why didn't she see the signs of civilization directly below her on a clear, cloudless day? It's almost as if she was caught in some kind of time distortion. Like she was seeing the island from a previous incarnation, decades or perhaps centuries before, but the modern-day inhabitants could see her clearly through the multidimensional fog.

In the following years, the cases of missing planes continued unabated:

1967: A Chase YC-122, carrying four persons en route to Grand Bahama from Palm Beach, Florida, vanished at some point northwest of Bimini on January 11th. The Chase Avitruc often operated a cargo flight between Fort Lauderale and Bimini in the Bahamas. It was transporting cargo for the production of a movie. It failed to arrive at Bimini and a search plane reported seeing pieces of wreckage off Bimini.[21]

1973: On June 1, a private pilot named Reno Rigoni disappeared with his copilot, Bob Corner, in a Cessna 180. No wreckage was found anywhere in the vicinity of his indicated flight pattern in a search which included the Everglades. No distress signal was heard from the radio.

1974: According to Berlitz, another unusual disappearance took place 900 miles southwest of the Azores on February 17. Thomas Gatch, an aspiring transatlantic balloonist on test flight, disappeared after radioing in his position.

And on it went. More recently, the cases have continued, but with perhaps better explanations (excuses) being offered.

1991: A Grumman Cougar light plane piloted by John Verdi, a retired Marine pilot, simply disappeared on a trip to Tallahassee, Florida while ascending to 29,000 feet. One second it was seen on the radar scopes, the next second it was gone with no sign of debris or wreckage found after an intense, four-day search.

2005: June 20, A Piper-PA-23 disappeared between Treasure Cay Island, Bahamas and Fort Pierce, Florida. There were three people on board.

2007: April 10, A Piper PA-46-310P disappeared near Berry Island after flying into a Level-6 thunderstorm and losing altitude. Two fatalities were listed.

2017: February 23, The Turkish Airlines flight TK183 (an Airbus A330-200) was forced to change its direction from Havana, Cuba to Washington Dulles airport after some mechanical and electrical problems occurred over the Triangle.

2017: May 15, A private MU-2B aircraft was at 24,000 feet when it vanished from radar and radio contact with air

An old print of waterspouts from *The Philosophy of Storms*, 1841.

traffic controllers in Miami. Plane wreckage was found.

And so it continues.

Earlier authors have intimated that, while the US government's official position is that nothing unusual is going on in the Bermuda Triangle, officials will tell you off the record that there is a danger in the area. John Godwin (author of *This Baffling World*), notes that American and British authorities never officially proclaimed the Triangle area to be a "danger zone" but "privately both marine and aviation experts have confessed that they may be facing a phenomenon of environment rather than a chain of technical mishaps." The question is, what is the unusual aspect of the environment of the Triangle that we are dealing with?

Perhaps that part of the mystery is best explained—or at least described—by the story told by private pilot Bruce Gernon. According to his story, as recited in his book *The Fog* (2005) and again in *Beyond the Bermuda Triangle* (2017), Gernon and his companions may be the only people to survive a direct encounter with the Triangle's famous "electronic fog" that seems to have swallowed up so many other aircraft. According to his account, Gernon encountered something mysterious shortly after taking off from Andros Island in the Bahamas on December 4, 1970, heading to Florida. This flight normally took one and a half hours in the Beechcraft Bonanza A36 plane he was flying, but thanks to a strange, unexplainable encounter with something unknown, that day Gernon made the trip in less than half that time.

Bruce Gernon.

First, Gernon encountered what he described as a lenticular cloud hovering lower than he had ever seen one before, just above the surface of the ocean. It quickly changed form to a "normal" looking cumulus cloud and was matching his 1,000 feet per minute climbing rate. Without warning, it seemed to expand and engulf his small aircraft, and after 10 minutes of climbing in and out of the cloud he finally broke free at 11,500 feet.

Gernon described the experience as a feeling of being chased and said that the behavior of the cloud felt "almost intelligent." He then leveled off and accelerated to 195 miles per hour, the Bonanza's maximum safe cruising speed, and was astonished when he checked behind him to see that cloud had once again reformed into an intense, dark squall of massive size that had reshaped itself into a semi-circular form behind him and was nearly encircling his aircraft. He estimated the size as at least 20 miles long.

Nearing the island of Bimini, Gernon then saw another, similar cloud forming in front of him, right in his flight path. This one was far more massive, at least 60,000 feet high, and extended all the way down to the surface, as the other cloud initially had. Checking with Miami control, he was informed that there was no significant weather on the radar between his plane and the Florida coast, so he decided that the storm must be relatively thin. With his passengers' agreement, he flew into the cloud and held his course.

What happened next is as astonishing as it is inexplicable.

> Upon entering the cloud we witnessed an uncanny spectacle. It became dark and black, without rain, and visibility was about four or five miles. There were no lightning bolts, only extraordinarily bright white flashes that would illuminate the entire surrounding area. The deeper we penetrated, the more intense the flashes became, so we made a 135-degree turn to the left and headed due south out of the cloud.
>
> We had been flying for 27 minutes. We thought we might be able to fly around the cloud, but after six or seven miles we saw that it continued in a near-perfect curve to the east. After two more minutes it became apparent that the cloud near Andros and the cloud near Bimini were actually opposite sides of the same ring-shaped body! The cloud must have formed just off of Andros Island and then rapidly spread outward into the shape of a doughnut with a diameter of 30 miles. This seemed impossible, but there was no other explanation. We were trapped inside a billowing prison, with no way under or over it.[22]

About 15 minutes later, Gernon saw what he described as a "U shaped" opening in the cloud, which he estimated at about 10

An illustration of Bruce Gernon's flight into the vortex.

A *Palm Beach Post* article on Bruce Gernon.

miles deep. He decided to head towards it to escape the cloud formation and as he approached, the "U" shaped shifted into a tunnel about one mile wide. As he got closer, he could see blue sky on the other side and also saw that the opening was rapidly narrowing. Accelerating beyond the safe speed of his Bonanza to over 230 mph, by the time he reached the gap it had narrowed to barely 200 feet across.

Now, however, he noted that the "tunnel" which had formed out of the cloud was only about one mile deep instead of the 10 miles he had originally estimated when he first saw it. Flying directly through it, he saw clouds swirling around his aircraft in a counterclockwise motion, and when he emerged at the other end he suddenly had a feeling of weightlessness and forward motion. He audibly gasped as he looked behind him and he saw the opening collapse and disappear.

When he looked around, he saw that all of his electronic instruments were malfunctioning, including his slowly spinning compass (even though the plane appeared to be stable and level) and he was surrounded by a gray fog instead of the blue sky he expected. Even though he estimated the visibility at more than two miles, he couldn't see land, sea or air. Just gray. Calling into Miami, he established contact and reported his position as 45 miles southeast of Bimini at about 10,500 feet flying west. Miami reported back that they could find no evidence of him in that area, but they did have an aircraft matching the Bonanza's signature directly over Miami Beach.

An illustration of Bruce Gernon's flight into the vortex.

Checking his watch, Gernon reported that he had been airborne only 34 minutes, and should be no closer to Miami than Bimini; they must be looking at another aircraft. These events had taken place over only about three minutes, and then suddenly the gray fog began to dissipate in what Gernon described as a very "electronic way," and the three men then found themselves out of the gray fog and in clear, sunny weather. Looking down, he saw the barrier island of Miami Beach and realized he was indeed over the city as the Miami tower had told him. Landing at Palm Beach, he checked the time and realized they had made the 75 minute trip in only 47 minutes, a complete impossibility. In order for that to be true, he would have had to travel more than 100 miles in distance in only three minutes.

What Gernon appears to have encountered is the same inexplicable "electronic fog" that so many others, including Flight 19, must have encountered. Except for some reason, Gernon kept his wits about him and avoided being swallowed up forever into some kind of space/time warp as the others had. Gernon's case, at least, appears to lend credence to the theory that there is some sort of odd physics operating in the Triangle, and that it may have played a role in so many of the mysterious disappearances that took place there. What we do not know yet, is just how that physics works. But we are getting there.

Of course, long before the Triangle was known for swallowing up planes in midair, it had a reputation for being something of a graveyard for shipping vessels and pleasure boats as well. Rarely the result of storms, most of these misadventures—like the aircraft disappearances—occurred in calm seas and clear weather. So before we consider the reality of the aerial "electronic fog" of the Triangle, we should look at the even longer record of mysterious happenings at sea in that area and the adjacent "Sargasso Sea." It, in some ways, is even more intriguing.

(Endnotes)

1 Berlitz, Charles (1974). *The Bermuda Triangle* (1st ed.). Doubleday.
2 Garner family records. Further information available upon request from dgarner@PacBell.net
3 https://www.vpnavy.com/vp2mem.html
4 https://www.bermuda-attractions.com/bermuda2_0000b1.htm
5 https://aviation-safety.net/database/record.php?id=19470703-0
6 https://www.bermuda-attractions.com/bermuda2_00009e.htm
7 https://en.wikipedia.org/wiki/BSAA_Star_Tiger_disappearance
8 https://en.wikipedia.org/wiki/BSAA_Star_Ariel_disappearance
9 Search for Star Ariel". *The Times*. 20 January 1949. p. 4.
10 "Accident investigation - minister - chief inspector - 1951 - 0458 - Flight Archive".
11 https://en.wikipedia.org/wiki/1948_Airborne_Transport_DC-3_(DST)_disappearance
12 Civil Aeronautics Board report
13 https://news.google.com/newspapers?nid=N2osnxbUuuUC&dat=19490105&printsec=frontpage
14 https://en.wikipedia.org/wiki/1953_Skyways_Avro_York_disappearance
15 https://www.bermuda-attractions.com/bermuda2_0000a0.htm
16 http://www.thequesterfiles.com/_pogo_22_--__the_bermuda_trian.html
17 http://www.mitchellgallery.org/flightlines/art/skyshield_winter88.pdf

18 https://www.airspacemag.com/history-of-flight/this-is-only-a-test-3119878/

19 http://www.thequesterfiles.com/_tyler_41__--__the_disappearan.html

20 Ranter, Harro and Fabian I. Lujan. "ASN Aircraft accident Fairchild C-119F-FA Flying Boxcar 51-2680 Bahamas." Aviation Safety Network, 2010. Retrieved: June 28, 2011.

21 https://aviation-safety.net/database/record.php?id=19670111-0

22 Gernon, Bruce and Rob MacGregor. *The Fog: A Never Before Published Theory of the Bermuda Triangle*. Llewellyn Publications, 2005.

Chapter 4

Mysterious Sea Disappearances

If the number of completely mysterious and unexplained disappearances of aircraft in the Bermuda Triangle is overwhelming—and we covered only the most famous cases—then the number of inexplicable sea ship cases is even more astonishing. Given that the modern aviation era only extends about as far back as World War II, if there was a true anomaly to the Bermuda Triangle mystery it would logically extend much further back than that. When it comes to the graveyard of the sea that is the Triangle, it certainly does.

The very first mention of an anomalous incident at sea in the Bermuda Triangle goes back literally as far as it can possibly go—all the way back to the first voyage of Christopher Columbus on his legendary journey to discover the New World. In that famous year of 1492 (more than 525 years ago), on the night of October 11, Columbus recorded a sighting of an impossible light at sea. Witnessed by the heroic explorer as well as the crew of the *Santa Maria* and members of the *Pinta* and *Nina* crews, Columbus recorded the incident in his log just days before his first landing at Guanahani. The light is reported in the *Diario* of Columbus as transcribed by Las Casas, then also in the *Historie* of Don Fernando (Columbus's second son, 1488-1539), the *Historia* of Oviedo (Spanish courtier, Crown official, and first chronicler of America, 1478-1557), the *Historia* of Bartolome de Las Casas and at least one proceeding of the *Pleitos Colombinos*, a lawsuit between the Crown and the heirs of Columbus. There is also a mention of it in the *Letters Patent* of May 24, 1493, awarding

Columbus an annuity for being the first to find land.[1]

According to Fernando's *Historie,* Columbus was the first to sight the light, which he thought might in fact be on land, but several others on the three ships also confirmed it:

> ...And this said, two hours before midnight, the Admiral being on the sterncastle, saw a light on land, but he says that it was a thing so occluded that he dares not affirm it might be land; still, he called one Pietro Guttieres, Credentiere to the Catholic King, and told him to look if he might see said light and he responded that he saw it, so immediately they called on Rodrigo Sanches de Segovia that he might look towards that part, but he could not see it because he did not climb up so quickly to where it might be seen. Nor did they see it thereafter, save once or twice; because of this they reckoned that it could be a candle or torch of fishermen or travelers who were raising and lowering the said light, or that haply they were passing from one house to another; whereas it disappeared and returned suddenly with such quickness, that few by this sign believed [it] to be near land.

Other translations of Columbus' *Diario* indicate that he described the light as "rising and falling," and not behaving at all like a fire on land. Given that there was no land in the area, it

Depiction of Columbus' USO encounter.

remains a complete mystery to this day exactly what Columbus actually witnessed. But what was soon clear was that it would not be the last mystery the Triangle had to offer ships at sea.

Obviously, it took centuries for a maritime travel industry to fully develop between Europe and the New World, and in that time there must have been considerable incidents of ships lost at sea in the Triangle that weren't recorded due to the primitive nature of record keeping. But once the modern era began, almost immediately the mysteries began to mount. A partial list of cases that have been considered mysteries of the Triangle includes:

1800: USS *Pickering*, on course from Guadeloupe to Delaware, lost with 90 people on board. (Possibly lost in a gale.)

1812: *Patriot* on her way from Charleston, South Carolina to New York City on December 30. Theodosia Burr Alston, daughter of Aaron Burr, was lost with her. (Possibly lost in a storm.)

1814: USS *Wasp*, last known position was the Caribbean, lost with 140 people on board. (Possibly lost in a storm.)

1824: USS *Wild Cat*, on course from Cuba to Tompkins Island, lost with 14 people on board (Possibly lost in a gale with 31 on board.)

1840: *Rosalie*, found abandoned except for a canary. (Possibly the "*Rossini*" found derelict.)

1881: The *Ellen Austin* is also found adrift in good order with no crew or signs of a struggle. Re-crewed, she's found again weeks later with the second crew missing.

1918: USS *Cyclops*, collier, left Barbados on March 4, lost with all 306 crew and passengers en route to Baltimore, Maryland.

1921: January 31, *Carroll A. Deering*, five-masted schooner, Captain W. B. Wormell, found aground and abandoned at Diamond Shoals, near Cape Hatteras, North Carolina.

1925: December 1, SS *Cotopaxi*, having departed Charleston, South Carolina two days earlier bound for

Havana, Cuba, radioed a distress call reporting that the ship was sinking. She was officially listed as overdue on 31 December.

1941: USS *Proteus* (AC-9), lost with all 58 persons on board in heavy seas, having departed St. Thomas in the Virgin Islands with a cargo of bauxite on 23 November. The following month, her sister ship USS *Nereus* (AC-10) was lost with all 61 persons on board, having also departed St. Thomas with a cargo of bauxite, on 10 December. According to research by Rear Admiral George van Deurs, USN, who was familiar with this type of ship from their service in the USN, the acidic coal cargo would seriously erode the longitudinal support beams, making these aging and poorly constructed colliers extremely vulnerable to breaking up in heavy seas. They were both sister ships of the USS *Cyclops*.

1958: *Revonoc*. A 43-foot racing yawl was lost with owner Harvey Conover and four others between Key West and Miami, Florida in a hurricane. The only trace found was the *Revonoc* 14-foot skiff near Jupiter, Florida.

1963: SS *Marine Sulphur Queen*, lost with 39 crewmen, having departed Beaumont, Texas, on 2 February with a cargo of 15,260 tons of sulphur. She was last heard from on 4 February, when she was in rough, nearly-following seas of 16 feet, with northerly winds of 25 to 46 knots, and listed as missing two days later. The Coast Guard subsequently determined that the ship was unsafe and not seaworthy, and never should have sailed. The final report suggested four causes of the disaster, all due to poor design and maintenance of the ship.

2015: In late July, two 14-year-old boys, Austin Stephanos and Perry Cohen, went on a fishing trip in their 19-foot boat. Despite an immediate 15,000 square nautical mile search by US Coast Guard, the pair's boat was found a year later off the coast of Bermuda, but the boys were never seen again.

2015: SS *El Faro* sank off of the coast of the Bahamas within the triangle on October 1. Search crews identified

Artist's rendering of the USS *Pickering* at the time of her commissioning.

the vessel 15,000 feet below the surface.

A breakdown of each of these cases leads one to an inevitable conclusion that is somewhat hard to believe but equally hard to dismiss.

The case of the USS *Pickering*, on course from Guadeloupe to Delaware, lost with 90 people on board in 1800 is generally the first cited case of the modern Triangle era. The *Pickering* was a topsail schooner in the United States Revenue Cutter Service (USRC) and then the United States Navy during the so-called "Quasi-War" with France.[2] She was named for Timothy Pickering, then the Secretary of State. The USRC *Pickering* was built at Newburyport, Massachusetts in 1798 for the Revenue Cutter Service. Captain Jonathan Chapman was her first commander. Commissioned into the Navy in July at the outbreak of the Quasi-War, she departed Boston on her first cruise on August 22, 1798. In 1799 and early 1800, she was part of Commodore Barry's squadron in the West Indies. Lieutenant Edward Preble commanded the *Pickering* from January through June 1799, when he was promoted to captain and took command of the frigate *Essex*.

Pickering was permanently transferred to the Navy on May 20, 1799 and re-designated the USS *Pickering*. Master Commandant Benjamin Hiller of the US Navy assumed command in June, and continued command of the ship for its final years. Under Hiller's command, the *Pickering* fought a notable engagement with the French privateer *L'Egypte Conquise* on October 18, 1799. The French ship was well fitted out and manned and should have been able to capture the *Pickering*. While the French ship carried fourteen 9-pound guns, four 6-pounders, and crew of 250, the American cutter had only fourteen 4-pounders and 70 men. After a nine-hour battle, however, the French ship was forced to surrender. The *Pickering* continued to cruise in the West Indies, and before her return to the United States had captured four French privateers, including *Voltigeuse, Atalanta, L'Active* and *Fly* and recaptured the American merchant ship *Portland*.

After her service in the war, the USS *Pickering* departed from Boston on June 10, 1800. Ordered to join Commodore Thomas Truxtun's squadron on the Guadeloupe Station in the West Indies, she sailed from New Castle, Delaware on August 20 directly into the Bermuda Triangle and was never heard from again. She is presumed by the Navy to have been lost with all hands in a gale in September, but this was never proven. The exact cause of the cutter's disappearance remains a mystery and is probably the earliest unexplained mystery involving the Triangle. This storm is also thought to have sunk USS *Insurgent*, a captured French frigate, which also vanished without a trace. According to Wikipedia, the *Insurgent* was lost in the same storm:[3]

> On 29 April 1800 Patrick Fletcher assumed command and was ordered to cruise between the West Indies and the American coast to protect American shipping interests and to capture any enemy vessels he encountered. *Insurgent* departed Baltimore 22 July and after a brief stop at Hampton Roads sailed for her station 8 August 1800. She was never heard from again, and the frigate and her crew were presumed lost during the severe storm that struck the West Indies on 20 September 1800.

The US Naval History and Heritage Command website tells generally the same story:[4]

> *Insurgent*, formerly the French frigate *L'Insurgente*, was captured by *Constellation*, Captain Thomas Truxtun in command, after a chase and battle of an hour and a quarter off the island of Nevis in the West Indies 9 February 1799. The battle was exceptionally well-fought under Truxtun's able leadership and remains one of the most famous in naval history. Considered a prize in the quasi-war with France, the frigate was refitted for service in the West Indies and cruised under Lt. John Rodgers in company with *Constellation* until May 1799.
>
> Ordered back to the United States, *Insurgent* was purchased by the Navy for $84,500. Commissioned with Captain Alexander Murray in command, *Insurgent* sailed from Hampton Roads for Europe 14 August 1799. Cruising in European waters during the winter of 1799-1800, the frigate captured French ship *Vendemaire* and recaptured the American ships *Margaret, Angora, Commerce,* and *William and Mary. Insurgent* returned to the United States in March 1800 via the West Indies.
>
> Patrick Fletcher assumed command of *Insurgent* on April 29, 1800 and was ordered to cruise between the West Indies and the American coast to see that United States shipping rights were observed and to capture any enemy vessels he encountered. *Insurgent* departed Baltimore 22 July and after a brief stop at Hampton Roads sailed for her station 8 August, 1800. Never heard from again, the frigate and her crew were presumed lost as a result of the severe storm which struck the West Indies 20 September 1800.

In 1812-13 the schooner *Patriot* disappeared on her way from Charleston, South Carolina to New York City. The ship was captained by the experienced William Overstocks, and was alleged to be carrying quite a bit of contraband that it had seized from ships of the naval blockade put up by the British in the War of

1812. *Patriot* was also carrying Theodosia Burr Alston, daughter of former Vice President Aaron Burr and the wife of Joseph Alston, governor of South Carolina. Why she was on board the ship is something of a mystery. According to at least one account, *Patriot* was a:

> ...famously fast ship which had originally been built as a pilot boat and had served as a privateer during the War of 1812 when it was commissioned by the United States government to prey on English shipping. She had been refitted in December, 1812 in Georgetown, her guns dismounted and hidden below decks. Her name was painted out and any indication of recent activity was entirely erased.

If *Patriot* had encountered any British military vessels, she would have been basically defenseless.[5]

Historians argue that she encountered a storm at sea and sank, but there is virtually no evidence to support this conclusion. Other accounts claim that she was captured by pirates and that Burr's daughter was forced to walk the plank or sold as a sex slave to other pirates. Burr himself bought into the shipwreck explanation, although there is no record of any severe storm or notable gale which might have caused the otherwise seaworthy ship to sink. No wreckage was ever found, and the body of Burr's daughter was never recovered. What happened to *Patriot* has never been adequately explained or even remotely ascertained. She simply vanished.

Another case frequently attributed to the Triangle was the 1814 disappearance of the USS *Wasp*. Her last known position was in the Caribbean with a crew of 140 men on board. According to the blog Bermuda Triangle Central,[6] the *Wasp* was a much-feared warship that wreaked havoc on British merchant marine shipping for months before her disappearance. *Wasp* apparently was quite a thorn in the British side during the war of 1812 (which lasted until 1815), having sunk the British ships *Three Brothers* and *Bacchus* and captured the 8-gun brig *Atlanta* in the course of a few months. After her capture, *Atlanta* was re-crewed with

The USS *Wasp*.

Wasp's sailors under the command of a Midshipman Geisinger and sent back to the United States. When she made port in Savannah, Georgia on November 4, 1814, Geisinger was surprised to learn that nothing had been heard from the *Wasp* since he had parted with the captured British ship. *Wasp* had been spotted by a Swedish merchantman sailing to England in the Caribbean, where she engaged and severely damaged a British frigate about two hundred miles northwest of the Cape Verde Islands. Two more English frigates were sent to hunt *Wasp* down, and they sighted her in the Triangle and began a pursuit, only to have her simply vanish into the mist overnight. When the sun set, the two British ships were in the process of running *Wasp* down. When the sun rose, *Wasp* was gone and there had been no storm or rough seas. She was never heard from again.

In 1824 a small two-masted, 48-ton displacement schooner named USS *Wild Cat* vanished while on course from Cuba to Tompkins Island in the West Indies. *Wild Cat* carried a crew of 31 and was tasked with ridding the shipping lanes of rampant piracy which was sweeping the Caribbean at that time. Captained by a Lieutenant Legare', *Wild Cat* is officially listed as "lost in gale" along with sister ships USS *Lynx* and USS *Hornet* but once again, there is no proof that any storm had a role in their disappearance. More likely, they might have encountered pirate vessels, but such victories were widely celebrated by the pirates in those days, and there is no account listing any encounters that might have led to their sinking.

One of the strangest cases is that of the *Rosalie/Rossini*, found abandoned and adrift in 1840 except for a cat and some birds which were the only living creatures onboard. The London *Times* reported the following: "Nov. 6, 1840—the *Rosalie*, a large French ship, bound from Hamburg to Havana—abandoned ship—no clue to an explanation. Most of the sails set—no leak—valuable cargo. There was a half-starved canary in a cage." The full article went on to quote from a letter, detailing the mysterious discovery:

SHIP DESERTED—A letter from Nassau, in the Bahamas, bearing date the 27th of August, has the following narrative:—A singular fact has taken place within the last few days. A large French vessel, bound from Hamburgh to the Havannah, was met by one of our small coasters, and was discovered to be completely abandoned. The greater part of her sails were set, and she did not appear to have sustained any damage. The cargo, composed of wines, fruits, silks, &c., was of very considerable value, and was in a most perfect condition. The captain's papers were all secure in their proper place. The soundings gave three feet of water in the hold, but there was no leak whatever. The only living beings found on board were a cat, some fowls, and several canaries half dead with hunger. The cabins of the officers and passengers were very elegantly furnished, and everything indicated that they had been only recently deserted. In one of them were found several articles belonging to a lady's toilet, together with a quantity of ladies' wearing apparel thrown hastily aside, but not a human being was to be found on board. The vessel, which must have been left within a very few hours, contained several bales of goods addressed to different merchants in Havannah. She is very large, recently built, and called the

Rosalie. Of her crew no intelligence has been received. (*Times* (London), November 6, 1840, p. 6, col. 3.)

Immediately, a controversy arose when it was discovered that there was no such ship as the *Rosalie* listed in any shipping manifest or Lloyd's of London list of insured vessels. Lloyds did have a listing for a ship named the *Rossini*, which also was listed as sailing from Hamburg Germany to Havana, just like the mysterious *Rosalie*.

J. F. Lane, an Assistant Shipping Editor for Lloyd's sent a letter to a Bermuda Triangle researcher named Lawrence Kusche in 1973 which explained what records could be found:

I regret that a search of Lloyd's Records has failed to reveal mention of any incident involving a vessel named *Rosalie* in the Bahamas in 1840. However, I am enclosing extracts from Lloyd's Records, which contain references to a vessel named *Rossini*, which would appear to be the vessel in which you are interested.

Given that most communications in 1840 were handwritten notes, it has been assumed that the author of the London *Times* article simply misread the ship's name on the letter he referenced in his story. However, the Lloyd's material on the *Rossini* contains conflicting information:

Lloyds List, September 25, 1840: Havana, 18th Aug. The *Rossini*, from Hambro to this port, struck on the Muares (Bahama Channel) 3rd inst.; Crew and Passengers saved." The other note reads "Lloyd's List, October 17, 1840: Havana, 5th Sept. The *Rossini*, from Hambro to this port, which struck on the Muares (Bahama Channel) 3rd ult. was fallen in with abandoned, 17th ult. and has been brought into this port a derelict. [7]

So while both notes assume that the name of the ship was *Rossini*, not *Rosalie*, one report says that the "crew and passengers were saved," while the other lists the ship, recovered on a different day, as "abandoned." It's clear that all three reports are describing the same vessel, but the condition of the ship and crew, date of discovery and ultimate disposition are all in conflict. Since two out of the three reports list the ship as empty, I'm going to accept that version of events and put the *Rosalie/Rossini* square into the category of the unexplained. It is also the first known case of a ship being found without its crew in the Triangle, although there would be many more in the coming century and a half.

However, Bermuda Triangle investigator Gian W. Quasar has found evidence that there were indeed two ships that were found derelict in the Bermuda Triangle in 1840 that sailed from Hamburg. One named the *Rossini*, and one named the *Rosalie*. "The British Maritime Museum does hold a record of her [*Rosalie*]. She was built in 1838, of 222 tons," he writes. So indeed, there were two ships that attempted to sail from Hamburg to Havana, and both ended up as derelicts under mysterious circumstances.

Gee, what a coincidence...

This also ties into one of the most famous and controversial cases of the Bermuda Triangle, the mystery of the *Ellen Austin* 40 years later.

According to legend, a sailing ship named the "*Ellen Austin*" (which may or may not have existed) found a derelict vessel in the Bermuda Triangle and placed a crew on board to sail the vessel to port. There are two versions of what happened to the vessel. One is that it was subsequently lost in a storm, the other is that the *Ellen Austin* lost sight of it in a "fog" (sound familiar?) and it was found a second time without the replacement crew. Author Lawrence David Kusche (*The Bermuda Triangle Mystery—Solved*) found no mention in 1880 or 1881 newspapers of this alleged incident, but he did trace the legend to a book by Rupert Gould called *The Stargazer Talks* published in 1943.

According to Gould:

> Last, and queerest of all, comes the case of the abandoned derelict, in seaworthy condition, which the British ship *Ellen Austin* encountered, in mid-Atlantic, in the year 1881. She put a small prize-crew on board the stranger, with instructions to make for St. John's,

Newfoundland, where she was bound herself.

The two ships parted company in foggy weather—but a few days later they met again. And the strange derelict was once more deserted. Like their predecessors, the prize-crew had vanished—forever. (Gould, p. 30.)

Numerous researchers stated that like the *Rosalie/Rossini*, all the sails were properly folded or tucked away, nothing was disturbed and there was no sign of a fight with pirates or any other conflict on board. They then go on to list numerous other facts found by numerous other researchers, like the fact that the *Ellen Austin*'s captain was named "Baker," or that she was alternatively bound for New York or Boston.

Later embellishments by Berlitz claimed that a second "prize crew" was placed aboard the derelict, and that it too was found later minus this second crew. This led to decades-long claims by skeptics that the *Ellen Austin* did not even exist and the whole story was a fabrication, but once again a check of Lloyd's of London records by Quasar proved the existence of a ship named the *Meta*, built in 1854, which was subsequently renamed the *Ellen Austin* in 1880.

The *Ellen Austin*.

According to Wikipedia, there were no casualty listings for any vessel either in 1880 or 1881 that would suggest a large number of missing men had been placed on board such a derelict and subsequently lost.[8] The Bermuda Triangle Central blog (a skeptical site) argues that although Gould was a "serious researcher" and "didn't make it up," without knowing his source, his claims are just fairy tales. In the end, they claim that "Until someone finds a contemporary historical account of the incident, like in a newspaper, a logbook, or a casualty report, one has to assume that this story, fascinating as it may be, is nothing but a sailor's yarn run amuck [sic]."

However I must point out that the skeptics spent years arguing that the *Ellen Austin* didn't even exist, only to be proven wrong. Now their fallback position is that yes, the ship existed but because of discrepancies in the various sources' sets of facts (not uncommon for a 140-year-old story) it is now just a "sailor's yarn run amok." As I have found, most such "yarns" become well known because something very close to that story actually happened. At this point, the *Ellen* Austin must be regarded as far more than another *Flying Dutchman* sailor's yarn.

The next major ship disappearance associated with the Bermuda Triangle took place early in the 20th century. The USS *Cyclops* (AC-4) was the second of four Proteus-class colliers built for the United States Navy several years before World War I, all of which were ultimately ill-fated ships. Named for a primordial race of one-eyed giants from Greek mythology, she was the second US Naval vessel to bear the name. The *Cyclops* left Barbados on March 4, 2018 headed for Baltimore. She never arrived and the loss of the ship and her 306 passengers and crew without a trace is one of the most often-cited mysteries of the Bermuda Triangle.

The loss remains the single largest loss of life in US Naval history not directly involving combat (at least as far as is known.) As it was wartime, she was thought to have been captured or sunk by a German raider or submarine, because she was carrying 10,800 long tons of manganese ore used to produce munitions. But German authorities at the time, and subsequently, denied any knowledge of the vessel.[9] The Naval History & Heritage Command has stated she "probably sank in an unexpected storm" but as usual, no evidence other than wild speculation is offered in support of this explanation. She simply vanished and took 306 souls with her.

The *Cyclops* was launched on May 7, 1910 as a commercial ore carrier by William Cramp & Sons of Philadelphia and placed in service on November 7, 1910. Lieutenant Commander George Worley, Master, Naval Auxiliary Service, was in command. Operating with the Naval Auxiliary Service, Atlantic Fleet, she traveled in the Baltic from May until July 1911 to supply Second Division ships. Returning to Norfolk, Virginia, she operated on the East Coast from Newport, Rhode Island to the Caribbean, servicing the naval fleet. During the United States' occupation of Veracruz in Mexico in 1914–1915, she supplied ships on patrol there with coal and received the thanks of the US State Department for cooperation in evacuating refugees.

With the American entry into World War I, the *Cyclops* was commissioned on May 1, 1917, with Worley still in command. She joined a convoy for Saint-Nazaire, France, in June 1917, returning to the US in July. Except for a voyage to Halifax, Nova Scotia, she served along the East Coast until January 9, 1918, when she was assigned to the Naval Overseas Transportation Service. She

The USS *Cyclops* on the Hudson River in 1911.

then sailed to Brazilian waters to fuel British ships in the South Atlantic, receiving the thanks of the US State Department and Commander-in-Chief, Pacific.

The *Cyclops* put to sea from Rio on February 16, 1918, and ported in El Salvador on February 20. Two days later, she departed for Baltimore, Maryland, with no stops scheduled, carrying the manganese ore. Wikipedia reports that the ship was thought to be overloaded when she left Brazil, as her maximum capacity was 8,000 long tons. Before leaving port, Commander Worley had submitted a report that the starboard engine had a cracked cylinder and was not operative. This report was confirmed by a survey board, which recommended, however, that the ship be returned to the United States. She made an unscheduled stop in Barbados because the water level was over the Plimsoll line, indicating that it was overloaded, but investigations in Rio proved the ship had been loaded and secured properly. *Cyclops* then set out for Baltimore on March 4th, and was rumored to have been sighted on March 9th by the molasses tanker *Amolco* near Virginia.

The *Cyclops* never made it to Baltimore, and no wreckage of her has ever been found. Rumors at the time suggested that on March 10th, the day after the ship was rumored to have been sighted by

LOSS OF THE COLLIER "CYCLOPS."

There has been no more baffling mystery in the annals of the Navy than the disappearance last March of the U. S. S. *Cyclops*, Navy collier of 19,000 tons displacement, with all on board. Loaded with a cargo of manganese, with 57 passengers, 20 officers, and a crew of 213 aboard, the collier was due in port on March 13. On March 4 the *Cyclops* reported at Barbados, British West Indies, where she put in for bunker coal. Since her departure from that port there has not been a trace of the vessel, and long-continued and vigilant search of the entire region proved utterly futile, not a vestige of wreckage having been discovered. No reasonable explanation of the strange disappearance can be given. It is known that one of her two engines was damaged and that she was proceeding at reduced speed, but even if the other engine had become disabled it would have not had any effect on her ability to communicate by radio. Many theories have been advanced, but none that seems to account satisfactorily for the ship's complete vanishment. After months of search and waiting the *Cyclops* was finally given up as lost and her name stricken from the registry.

Excerpt from the US Navy annual report on the loss of the USS *Cyclops*.

Amolco, a violent storm swept through the Virginia Capes area, but there is no official record of this. This has led sceptics to conclude that the combination of the overloaded condition, engine trouble, and bad weather were the reason *Cyclops* sank. But let me emphasize: there is no evidence at all that *Cyclops* sank! No wreck, no bodies, no mounds of ore on the sea bottom. In fact, there is just as much evidence that she was beamed to Mars as there is that she "sank." An exhaustive naval investigation agreed, concluding: "Many theories have been advanced, but none that satisfactorily accounts for the ship's complete vanishment" [9]

On June 1, 1918, Assistant Secretary of the Navy Franklin D. Roosevelt (yes, the future president) declared *Cyclops* to be officially lost and all hands deceased. In 1918, a short summary of the loss of *Cyclops* was listed in the US Navy Annual Report.[10]

Subsequently, two of *Cyclops'* three sister ships also mysteriously disappeared in the Bermuda Triangle, in what seems more than a simple coincidence. The USS *Proteus* (AC-9) was sold on March 8, 1941, became part of the Canadian Merchant Navy, and was lost at sea without a trace, probably in or near the Caribbean Sea, sometime after November 25, 1941. USS *Nereus* (AC-10) was sold to the Aluminum Company of Canada on February 27, 1941. She was lost without a trace after departing Saint Thomas, US Virgin Islands, on December 10, 1941, with a load of bauxite ore for making aluminum. The 4th ship in the group, the USS *Jupiter*, was converted to an aircraft carrier during the war and was recommissioned the USS *Langley* (CV-1.) She was stationed in the Philippines in December 1941 and departed for Australia following the Japanese attacks on Pearl Harbor and the Philippines. On February 27, 1942, while ferrying fighter planes to Southeast Asia, she was attacked by Japanese aircraft and was hit by five bombs, causing critical damage. After her surviving crewmembers were rescued, *Langley/Jupiter* was scuttled by torpedoes fired by her escorting destroyers.

Years later, Rear Admiral George van Deurs suggested that the loss of *Cyclops* could be owing to structural failure, as her sister ships suffered from issues where the I-beams that ran the length of the ship had eroded due to the corrosive nature of some of the cargo carried. For a BBC Radio 4 documentary, reporter Tom

Mangold had an expert from Lloyd's of London investigate the loss of the *Cyclops*. The expert noted that manganese ore, being much denser than coal, had room to move within the holds even when fully laden.

Furthermore, the hatch covers were canvas, and when wet, the ore can become a slurry. As such, the load could shift and cause the ship to list. Combined with a possible loss of power from its one engine, it could founder in bad weather.[11]

The reality, however, is that there is no evidence of "bad weather" in any of the three ships' disappearances, no evidence that the cargo got wet, and therefore no reason to conclude that this theory is valid. As to Admiral van Deurs' suggestion that structural failure could have occurred, it is based only on the fact that a "similar" ore-carrying ship (the USS *Jason*) was known to have snapped in two in calm seas when overloaded during the war. This ignores the fact, however, that *Jason's* design wasn't really all that similar, and the fact that the *Jason*, the *Proteus* and the *Nereus* had all been in service some *22 years* beyond the disappearance of the *Cyclops*, making "erosion" of structural beams on the much younger ship an unlikely explanation to say the least.

The fact that three of the four doomed ships were lost in the Bermuda Triangle seems to be a coincidence of epic proportions, and a far more likely factor in their disappearance than the I-beam erosion. To this point, the loss of the *Cyclops* still has a well-earned place in the lore of the Triangle.

One of the more famous and yet misreported modern cases is the disappearance on December 1, 1925 of the SS *Cotopaxi* in the Triangle. The *Cotopaxi* was a 2,351-ton-displacement tramp steamer built in 1918 by the Great Lakes Engineering Works in Ecorse, Michigan. She was headed from Charleston, South Carolina to Havana, Cuba laden with a full load of coal when she disappeared with a crew of 32 on board. The *Cotopaxi* set sail on November 29, and two days out, on December 1, there was a report of a distress signal from the boat indicating she was listing and taking on water during a tropical storm. However, the only reports of this "tropical storm" with winds "probably reaching hurricane force" are from two obscure newspapers of the period, the Lawrence, Kansas *Journal World*, which reported the storm,

The SS *Cotopaxi*.

and the Spokane, Washington *Spokesman-Review*, which reported the alleged distress signal.[12,13]

Neither is a major newspaper, and if a tropical storm hit Florida around that time, why wasn't it reported in a Florida newspaper? The truth is, the *Cotopaxi* was listed as overdue on December 31, 1925 and simply was never verifiably heard from again after she steamed away from Charleston on November 29. Also, no other ships are mentioned in any reports from the period as having been lost in the Triangle during that period, despite the alleged presence of this "tropical storm." It's easy to conclude from this that there most likely wasn't one. The truth is, no one knows what happened to her.

The case gained great fame in the 1979 film *Close Encounters of the Third Kind* when director Steven Spielberg used it in a dramatic opening scene where the "wreck" of the *Cotopaxi* is found thousands of miles away from the Triangle in the Gobi desert, absent its crew. Presumably, it was placed there by extraterrestrials as a signal that they are about to make themselves known.

The *Cotopaxi* didn't make the news again until the fall of 2018 when a spoof website called "World News Daily Report" ran an article saying the ship had been found over 90 years after its disappearance adrift in Cuban waters with no crew.[14] It breathlessly reported:

111

The Cuban Coast Guard announced this morning, that they had intercepted an unmanned ship heading for the island, which is presumed to be the SS *Cotopaxi*, a tramp steamer which vanished in December 1925 and has since been connected to the legend of the Bermuda Triangle.

The Cuban authorities spotted the ship for the first time on May 16, near a restricted military zone, west of Havana.

THINK SHIP TYPHOON WRECK

Abandon Hope for Crew of 30 on C topaxi.

KEY WEST, Fla., Dec. 7. (*AP*)— Virtually all hope has been abandoned for the finding of the steamer Cotopaxi, which left Charleston November 29 bound for Havana with a cargo of coal and which has not been heard from since last Tuesday when S. O. S. signals were received from the vessel, it was revealed here tonight after an exhaustive search from Norfolk to Cuba by coast guard vessels.

It is believed the steamer fell a victim to the tropical storm, although there is the possibility that members of her crew, numbering 30 men, were picked up by a passing vessel.

The hope that the crew was saved is only slight, however.

Newspaper clipping from the December 8, 1925 edition of the Spokane, Washington, *Spokesman Review* newspaper.

They made many unsuccessful attempts to communicate with the crew and finally mobilized three patrol boats to intercept it.

When they reached it, they were surprised to find that the ship was actually a nearly 100-year old steamer identified as the *Cotopaxi*, a name famously associated with the legend of the Bermuda Triangle.

An exhaustive search of the ship led to the discovery of the captain's logbook.

It then went on to quote a real person, General Abelardo Colomé Ibarra:

> The Vice President of Council of Ministers, General Abelardo Colomé, announced that the Cuban authorities were going to conduct a thorough investigation to elucidate the mystery of the ship's disappearance and reappearance.
>
> "It is very important for us to understand what happened," says General Colomé.

The article and several others included pictures of what certainly could have been the rusted-out hull of the *Cotopaxi*, which may have been lost in the interdimensional fog for nearly a century. If the picture, but not the article, is authentic, then it raises some other interesting questions. Was the report actually true? Did the Cubans suddenly discover the lost wreck of the *Cotopaxi*? Was the fake news article just a way of getting the information out, but

The SS *Cotopaxi*, as seen in the film *Close Encounters of the Third Kind*.

113

with plausible deniability? Certainly, there isn't much in the way of evidence supporting the tropical storm theory besides a couple of obscure news articles published thousands of miles away from the Florida coast. So what actually happened to the boat?

Fortunately, this is a case in which I have some personal experience and expertise. In August of 2017, I was hired along with my friend Steve Doran and couple of other cast members to shoot a "sizzle reel" for a proposed show on the Science Channel about the Triangle. We flew to Jacksonville, got set up and proceeded to shoot a complete segment on one case associated with the Bermuda Triangle. The case they chose was the disappearance of the *Cotopaxi*. What we discovered was that there was a wreck well off the coast of Florida that had been found by a local diver that was a good candidate for being the wreck of the *Cotopaxi*.

The diver had found the wreck in over 30 feet of water and recovered some items from it including a brass pump, a brass porthole with the glass still intact and several other instruments. They dated from the time of the *Cotopaxi*'s construction and were stamped with serial numbers that indicated they were manufactured by Michigan shops local to the *Cotopaxi*'s construction yard. This would be expected if they came from a subcontractor of the Great Lakes Engineering Works, which built her.

The wreck was, however, significantly due east of the shipping lanes that *Cotopaxi* would have used, raising the question of

Alleged picture of the wreck of the *Cotopaxi*.

whether it was the same ship. However, had there actually been a significant tropical storm, she could have easily been blown off course by that storm. Lastly, the wreck was found with large piles of coal all around it, which was of course the ship's cargo. These and other clues led me to believe that the diver had in fact found the wreckage of the *Cotopaxi*, finally solving the mystery of what happened to her and her crew of 32.

I must stress, however, that this is simply my opinion at the time of this writing. Until we find a barge board or a name plate with the name "*Cotopaxi*" etched on it, we have no proof the shipwreck has been found. Maybe some day.

At this point, I'd say we have firmly established that there is enough of a mystery around the lore of the Triangle to move on from the question of whether there is something to the Bermuda Triangle to the question of what could be the explanation for it. What could cause a B-52 to simply disappear in mid-flight during a military training exercise? How does a group of experienced Navy pilots "get lost" on a simple training mission? What could cause the mysterious "electronic fog" reported so often in the Triangle, where the comforting "laws of physics" themselves seem to short out? Well, I think I have an answer, and it may surprise you.

(Endnotes)

1 https://web.archive.org/web/20080907085314/http://www.millers-ville.edu/~columbus/data/art/MARVEL01.ART

2 https://en.wikipedia.org/wiki/Quasi-War

3 https://en.wikipedia.org/wiki/USS_Insurgent

4 https://www.history.navy.mil/research/histories/ship-histories/danfs/i/insurgent.html

5 http://bermudatrianglecentral.blogspot.com/2010/08/patriot.html

6 http://bermudatrianglecentral.blogspot.com/2010/08/uss-wasp.html

7 J. F. Lane, Assistant Shipping Editor, Lloyd's, letter to Kusche, August 15, 1973, in Kusche, *Bermuda Triangle Mystery*, p. 25

8 https://en.wikipedia.org/wiki/List_of_Bermuda_Triangle_incidents

9 https://en.wikipedia.org/wiki/USS_Cyclops_(AC-4)

10 United States Navy Dept (1918.) Annual Reports of the Navy Department: Report of the Secretary of the Navy. Miscellaneous reports. US Government Printing Office.
11 Mangold, Tom, "Inside the Bermuda Triangle: the Mysteries Solved," BBC Radio 4 2009.
12 Lawrence *Journal-World*, December 1, 1925. p.1
13 The *Spokesman-Review,* December 8, 1925. p.2 "Think Ship Typhoon Wreck"
14 https://worldnewsdailyreport.com/bermuda-triangle-ship-reappears-90-years-after-going-missing/

Chapter 5

The Physics of the Triangle

So without question, the potential exists for a deep and abiding mystery in the Bermuda Triangle. As we have seen, all signs point to a mysterious and unexplainable force operating in the Triangle that doesn't exist in other parts of the world. At least, as far as we know. But until now, there has never been a specific theory about what that force might be or where it comes from. We've all heard about the lost crystals of Atlantis, buried 20,000 leagues under the sea and still sporadically operating and creating waves of time-space distortion and creating the long reported "fogs," electronic and otherwise, that swallow up ships and planes. But what is the truth of that? Are submerged alien spacecraft creating rogue waves that sweep away ships? Are methane emissions sucking ships into funnels that swallow them whole? Or does physics simply operate differently in the Triangle? Or is there something even more hidden and surprising at the heart of the mystery of the Triangle?

The answer is yes, there is. And it comes from a surprising source millions of miles from Earth. It comes from a set of arcane ruins on the surface of Mars.

I first read about the hyperdimensional physics model of the universe in Richard C. Hoagland's book *The Monuments of Mars* in the early 1990s. The name comes from the simple idea that everything we see and experience in this universe as energy actually originates from somewhere else—from outside our observable 3D realm. The word "hyperspace," from which the term "hyperdimensional physics" is derived, was first coined in 1854 by the German mathematician Georg Riemann. He wrote the first mathematical science paper actually describing the geometry of a spatial dimension—the 4th—beyond this one. From then on, in the language of science anyway, higher dimensions were collectively lumped together and referred to as "hyperspace."

As I wrote with Richard in my first book *Dark Mission*:

> The cornerstone of the hyperdimensional model is the notion that higher spatial dimensions not only exist, but are also the underlying foundation upon which our entire 3D reality exists. Beyond that, everything in our observable 3D world is, in fact, driven by mathematically modeled "information transfer" from these higher dimensions. This information transfer might simply be the result of changes in the geometry of a connected system, say a change in the orbital parameters of a planet, like Jupiter or the Earth. Since we are limited in our perceptions to the 3D universe we live in, we cannot "see" these higher dimensions. However, we can see (and measure) changes in these higher dimensions that have a simultaneous effect on our reality. By definition, this change in higher dimensional geometry is perceived in our 3D universe as an 'energy output'…

In other words, when planets and stars and even whole galaxies change their positions relative to each other, these actions create "a tremor in the Force" in higher, imperceptible dimensions. Because these resonant waves aren't restricted by our limited three-dimensional "laws" like the supposedly fixed speed of light, they can (and demonstrably do) have an effect in our universe at great distances—and instantaneously. This single notion (instantaneous action at a distance) in and of itself completely undercuts all our current models of reality, which are based on the very inadequate "Laws of Physics" that scientists feel compelled to follow.

In *The Monuments of Mars* and in an earlier paper entitled "The Message of Cydonia," Hoagland and his co-researcher Erol Torun argued that certain mathematical alignments of what appeared to be ancient ruins on the planet Mars (yep, I said it) seemed to be implying that there was an unknown or previously undiscovered Force operating in the universe. This Force left distinct signatures all over the solar system in the form of energetic upwellings found on almost all the major planets very near the latitude of 19.5 degrees. Neptune's Great Dark Spot, the Great Red Spot of Jupiter, the erupting volcanoes of Jupiter's moon Io, Olympus Mons on Mars (which is the largest shield volcano in the solar system) and Earth's own Maunakea volcano in Hawaii all were at, or very near, the 19.5° latitude. They later realized that the location of these energy upwellings were based on the geometry of a circumscribed tetrahedron, basically a four-sided pyramid surrounded by a sphere.

This single numeric clue led Hoagland and Torun to the early research of John Clerk Maxwell and also to a group of rogue mathematicians called topologists. They found that the topologists had done a great deal of theoretical research mapping the mathematical properties of a rotating "hypersphere"—a sphere that exists in more than just our standard three spatial dimensions.

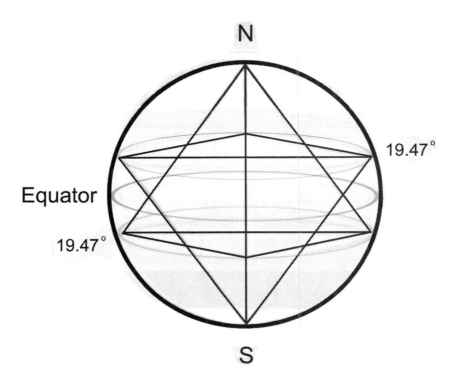

Two tetrahedrons circumscribed by a sphere.

The arcane math describing this "hypersphere" and the multiple dimensions (26) above it are so complex that they are virtually unintelligible to all but the most educated math buffs. But the math also said that the signatures of the higher dimensional states of this sphere would be observable here in its primitive, three-dimensional state. If the hypersphere was rotating (and remember, everything in our universe is rotating at all times), then the math required that rotating, roiling, twisting motions, exactly like the observed rotational dynamics of Jupiter's Great Red Spot, would leave a marker on the sphere in 3D at a specific location: 19.5 degrees latitude.

In other words, if you take a sphere, like oh I don't know, a planet say, and you rotate it, then you will pull energy from the higher state of the planet (the hypersphere), and that energy will preferentially "upwell" from inside the planet according to the geometry of a tetrahedron encased in a sphere, and appear at or around 19.5 degrees. This is exactly what Hoagland and Torun observed all over the solar system. As they went even deeper into the math, it implied that the tetrahedron is even more than that; it's nothing less than the base building block of all the solid matter in the physical three-dimensional universe that we live in. In fact, tetrahedrons are used by video game programmers all over the world to create all the 3D objects in the games you play because they have found that this is the easiest way to build solid objects in 3D. There is also a certain kind of balance in the symbolic nature of the geometry of a tetrahedron circumscribed by a sphere, since the tetrahedron is the simplest of all solid geometric forms (the so-called Platonic solids) and the sphere is the most complex.

The backstory on all this is absolutely fascinating, and directly connected to the Ancient Alien visitor theory.

In the midst of the first serious Cydonia Mars investigation in 1988, Hoagland was approached by Torun, a cartographer and satellite imagery interpreter for the Defense Mapping Agency. Given his specific scientific training and working experience, Torun was probably the most uniquely qualified person on the planet to render a judgment on the potential artificiality of the Cydonia enigmas. After attaining a degree in geology with a specialty in geomorphology, he had spent more than 10 years of his professional life looking at remote sensing imagery just like the original *Viking* data and distinguishing artificial structures from naturally occurring landforms. It was, in fact, his *job*.

After reading *Monuments*, he had written Hoagland expressing his surprise that his initial assumptions about the subject were not supported by his subsequent analysis. He was particularly impressed with the geometry and geology of the D&M Pyramid. "I have a good background in geomorphology and know of no mechanism to explain its formation," he wrote Hoagland. Torun had come to the Mars investigation as a skeptic, relatively certain he would find that the geomorphic interpretations and the early

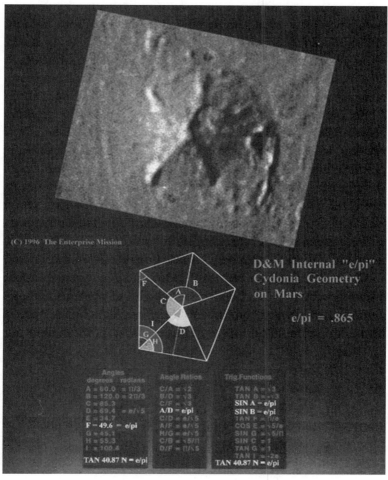

The geometry of the D&M Pyramid.

contextual alignments cited by Hoagland would turn out to be "false positives" in the search for answers to the riddle of Cydonia. Yet, once he had a chance to study the Cydonia images in detail, Torun concluded that the D&M itself was nothing less than the "Rosetta Stone" of Cydonia, finding a series of significant mathematical constants expressed in the internal geometry of the D&M. Being careful to avoid projecting his own biases on the measurements, Torun decided beforehand that he would restrict his analysis to just a few possible relationships.

As it turned out, not only did the D&M *have* a consistent internal geometry, it was also one full of rich geometric clues that spoke to him of a mathematical message coded with intent. He found numerous repetitive references to specific mathematical constants, like e/π, $\sqrt{2}$, $\sqrt{3}$, $\sqrt{5}$ and references to ideal hexagonal and pentagonal forms. He also found geometry linking the shape of the D&M to other ideal geometric figures, like the Golden Ratio (ϕ) and the *Vesica Piscis*, which is the root symbol of the Christian church, and the five basic "Platonic Solids"—the tetrahedron, cube, octahedron, dodecahedron and icosahedron. Further studies found that the reconstructed shape of the D&M, as determined by Torun *before* he took any of the measurements, is the only one that could produce this specific set of constants and ratios. More than that, these same constants showed up redundantly in all the different methods of measurement, and were not dependent on terrestrial methods of measurement (i.e., a radial measurement system based on a 360° circle). As Torun put it: "All of this geometry is 'dimensionless;' i.e., it is not dependent on such cultural conventions as counting by tens, or measuring angles in the 360 system. This geometry will 'work' in any number system."

Torun also discovered that the latitude of his reconstructed apex of the D&M was 40.868, which was a very close fit for the arctangent of the e/π ratio. Torun concluded that this was most likely an intended clue to anyone studying the structure that it was artificial. Such a self-referential numeric connection was, in his opinion, quite unlikely to occur by chance. Put simply, the D&M "knows where it is" on the surface of Mars.

After receiving Torun's study, Hoagland quickly realized that they were on the verge of a potentially important discovery. If

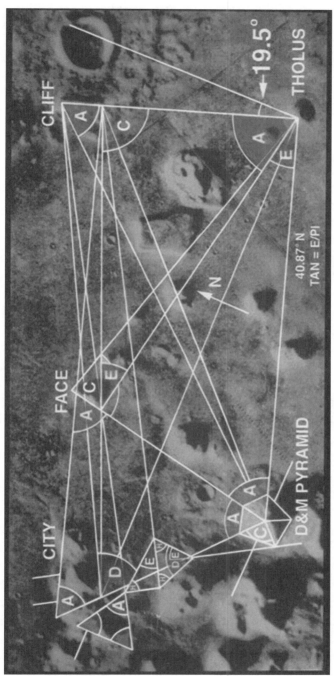

Hoagland's Cydonia "Geometric Relationship Model."

Torun's numbers were repeatable throughout the Cydonia Complex, if the same angles and ratios appeared in the larger relationships between the already established potential "monuments," then they would have a very strong argument that Torun's model was valid. Again being careful to only take measurements between obvious features (the apex of the Tholus and D&M, the straight line defined by the Cliff, the center of the City Square, the apex of the tetrahedral Crater Pyramid), Hoagland found that many of the same angles, ratios and trig functions applied all over the Cydonia Complex.

Somewhat stunned by what they had found, Hoagland and Torun had come to the realization that there was a message on the ground at Cydonia. The problem was that they didn't know what that message was trying to say.

In the message itself was the key to decoding it. One of the angles noted by Torun within the D&M was 19.5°, which occurred twice. Hoagland also found the same "19.5°" encoded in the broader Cydonia complex three more times. Searching for the significance of this number, they eventually determined that it related to the geometry of the tetrahedron. The simplest of the five so-called "Platonic Solids" (because it is the most fundamental three-dimensional form that can exist), it made a certain kind of sense to use this "lowest order" geometric shape as a basis for establishing communication across the eons.

If a tetrahedron is surrounded (circumscribed) by a sphere, with its apex anchored at either the North Pole or South Pole, then the three vertices of the base will "touch" the sphere at 19.5° in the hemisphere opposite the polar apex alignment. In addition, the value of e (as in the e/π ratio which is encoded at least ten times throughout the Cydonia complex) is 2.718282, a near exact match for the ratio of the surface area of a sphere to the surface area of a tetrahedron (2.720699).

This whole "tetrahedral" motif was reinforced when they went back to the original Cydonia images. Some of the small mounds Hoagland had noted earlier had the look of tetrahedral pyramids, and the Crater Pyramid, which is involved with one of the key 19.5 measurements, is also clearly tetrahedral. The mounds themselves were also arranged into a couple of sets of equilateral triangles, the

2D base figure for a tetrahedral pyramid.

Later, Dr. Horace Crater, an expert in probabilities and statistics, did a study of the mounds at Cydonia with Dr. Stanley McDaniel. What Crater found was that not only was there a non-random pattern in the distribution of nearly identical mounds at Cydonia, but that the pattern of distribution was overwhelmingly tetrahedral—and to a factor of 200 million to one against a natural origin.

In 1989, Hoagland and Torun proceeded to publish their results in a new paper titled, appropriately, "The Message of Cydonia." Based on the barrage of ad hominem criticism Hoagland had experienced after "Monuments" was published two years before, they assumed that it would be pointless to try to have their paper published in the NASA-controlled peer review press. Instead, they decided to go "straight to the people" and uploaded the paper to CompuServe, the largest online message board of its time.

The paper contained a number of predictions based on their evolving theory of the tetrahedral Message of Cydonia and also the even more radical new idea that within the tetrahedral mathematics was nothing less than an entirely new physics model. Hoagland then found that there was a long-abandoned line of thought by some of the masters of early physics, including James Clerk Maxwell, which included the idea that certain problems in electromagnetics could be solved by the imposition of higher spatial dimensions into the equations. The energies coming from these higher dimensions would then be "reflected" in our lower three dimensional universe through tetrahedral geometries. It was this crucial insight, they decided, that the builders of Cydonia were ultimately trying to impart.

The reductionists were quick to attack Hoagland and Torun's model. The critics argued against the validity of the model on one of two basic counts—that the measurements were either inaccurate, or if they were accurate, they did not mean what Hoagland and Torun implied they meant.

Anonymous memos from within NASA in the late 1980s used the same sorts of tactics they often do. They argued that Torun's measurements were not reliable because of the amount of error built into the ortho-rectified images. They frequently disputed the measurements themselves, but did not actually bother to try to reproduce them. Dr. Ralph Greenberg, a University of Washington mathematics professor, has more recently taken up this view. Greenberg has written several documents critical of Hoagland and Torun's model, and has also made something of a mini-career for himself accusing Hoagland of lying about his contributions to the idea of life under the oceans of Europa.

Dr. Michael Malin of Malin Space Science Systems (who controlled the camera for the then planned Mars Observer and the current Mars Global Surveyor) took a slightly different tack, agreeing that the measurements made by Hoagland and Torun "are not wholly in dispute" but arguing that even if the numbers were right, it did not necessarily follow that they meant something significant.

Most of these critiques are typical of the type of reaction you get from scientists when their established paradigms are threatened or when experts in particular fields try to apply the standards they are familiar with to a problem that is outside their experience. The issue of margins of error, especially, is one that (even today) is simply misunderstood, even by experienced mathematicians. Put simply, Greenberg argues—as many have before him—that the margin of error built into the measurements of the Cydonia Complex renders them useless, because they are large enough to make almost "any" mathematical constants and ratios possible. Greenberg, who has become pretty much the point man for attacks on the Cydonia Geometric Relationship Model, also claimed that Hoagland and Torun "selected" the angles they found, implying that they were looking for specific relationships before they ever started.

For the record, Greenberg also argues that the frequently cited mathematical and astronomical alignments of the Pyramids in Egypt are fallacious, even though few Egyptologists doubt them. It is by now well established that the base of the Great Pyramid is a square with right angle corners accurate to 1/20th of a degree. The side faces are all perfect equilateral triangles which align precisely with true north, south, east and west. The length of each side of the base is 365.2422 Hebrew cubits, which is the exact length of the solar year. The slope angle of the sides results in the pyramid having a height of 232.52 cubits. Dividing two times the side length by this height gives a figure of 3.14159. This figure (π) gives the circumference of a circle when multiplied by its diameter. The perimeter of the base of the pyramid is exactly equal to the circumference of a circle with a diameter twice the height of the pyramid itself.

Because of the angle of the slope sides, for every ten feet you ascend on the pyramid, your altitude is raised by nine feet. Multiplying the true altitude of the Great Pyramid by ten to the power of nine, you get 91,840,000, which is very nearly the distance from the sun to the Earth in miles. In addition, the builders also apparently knew the tilt of the Earth's axis (23.5°), how to accurately calculate degrees of latitude (which vary as an observer ventures farther from the equator) and the length of the Earth's precessionary cycle.

And all of this, according to the brilliant Dr. Greenberg, is just a coincidence. Just an example of what he called "the power of randomness."

Greenberg's arguments are pure reductionism. Forgetting for a moment the sheer unlikelihood of finding consistent and redundant mathematical linkages among a very few objects pre-selected only for their anomalous geology (which Greenberg does not address in any of his arguments) not for their possible mathematical relationships to one another, and using only clear and obvious structural points on these objects from which to measure, Greenberg completely fails to grasp the issue—Hoagland and Torun's measurements are nominal, meaning that they are valid to the closest fit of the methodology employed. They are not saying, "these are the numbers within a loose tolerance range," they are saying flatly "these are the numbers." The tolerances are just what we have to live with pending higher resolution images. Further, having stated that the measurements reflect a specific tetrahedral geometry—not just any set of "significant" mathematical numbers, as Greenberg implies—and that they encode a predictable physics, it becomes very easy to simply test their contextual model versus his reductionist view. Greenberg seeks to isolate the numbers themselves, and argue only his view of the "power of randomness," rather than simply test the alignments in the greater context of the physics they imply.

Fortunately, "The Message of Cydonia" contained two predictions that would provide the ideal opportunity to do just that. At that time, *Voyager 2* was approaching Neptune but had yet to image the planet up close. At the end of their paper, Hoagland and Torun put in three specific predictions about what *Voyager* would see. They predicted a storm or disturbance within a few degrees of the tetrahedral 19.5° latitude. Based on their further interpretation of the hyperdimensional physics they were developing, they also predicted that this disturbance would be in the southern hemisphere of the planet, and that the magnetic dipole polarity of Neptune's magnetic field would be anchored at the Northern Pole.

All three predictions—remember, based on the supposedly "fallacious" numbers derived from a supposedly "meaningless" set of alignments of possible ruins on Mars—turned out to be...

Absolutely correct.

Greenberg and the reductionists then argued "a single prediction, no matter what it is based on, cannot be relied upon as proof of anything." This tactic, combining the predictions into a single one instead of three, is a common means of dismissing the frequency of Hoagland and Torun's successes. As Harvard astronomer Halton Arp put it in his excellent book *Seeing Red*, "The game here is to lump all the previous observations into one 'hypothesis' and then claim there is no second, confirming observation."

There is, flatly, no way that Hoagland and Torun could use a set of "meaningless" or "fallacious" data to make three such accurate predictions about features on a planet the human race had never seen up close before. These features have no explanation in the conventional models, at least as far as providing a mechanism for the storm, the location of the storm, and its relationship to the magnetic pole of the planet. In other words, there is no way they could have just "gotten lucky" by using established models of the solar system. Their predictions come solely from the Cydonia Geometric Alignment model.

This is not only a ringing endorsement of the validity of both the measurements and the physics model deduced from them, but also a harsh indictment of the methods and motives of both

Greenberg and Malin (Greenberg at one point challenged Hoagland to a "debate" on the mathematics of Cydonia, but only if he could exclude Crater's tetrahedral mound data, which he acknowledged he could not explain away).

Armed with the suspicion that they had found the intent of the builders of the "Monuments of Mars," Hoagland and Torun now turned their attention to the possible application of the geometry they had discovered.

One of the first things Hoagland and Torun noticed was that throughout the observed solar system, planetary disturbances and upwellings of energy seemed to preferentially cluster around this key 19.5° latitude. As noted above, Neptune's Great Dark Spot (as it came to be known), the Great Red Spot of Jupiter, the erupting volcanoes of Jupiter's moon Io, Olympus Mons on Mars (the largest shield Volcano in the solar system) and Earth's own Maunakea volcano in Hawaii all were at, or very near, 19.5° latitude.

Beyond that, clusters of sunspots occurring from the heightened energy output of the sun during the peak of the solar cycle also centered around 19.5°. And interestingly, whether the upwelling event was located in the northern or southern hemisphere depended on the alignment of the body's magnetic field. If the field were anchored at the South Pole, the disturbance appeared at or around 19.5° in the northern hemisphere. Conversely, if it were anchored at the northern pole, the disturbance appeared in the south. It was as if there really were "giant tetrahedrons" inside the planets, driving the physics of these energy upwellings and forcing them to comply with some mysterious, unseen rules of behavior (of course, there aren't; it's actually a standing wave pattern of forces).

Let's take this even a bit further. If everything that is spinning (and remember, that's literally everything) is putting out energy, then doesn't it follow that these energetic forces might in fact interact with each other in some way? Might these waves of energy generated by the spin of the planets have some kind of impact on our physical reality here on Earth? It's an interesting notion. If only we had some way to prove it, right? Well...

In the 1950s, RCA hired a young engineer named John Nelson in an effort to improve the reliability of shortwave radio communications around the Earth. Such radio transmissions were crucial to long distance communications at the time because the high frequency signals could be bounced off the Earth's ionosphere, a layer of electrically charged ("ionized") atoms that lies between the upper atmosphere and the Earth's magnetic field. RCA requested the study because they had noticed that the quality of the shortwave transmissions varied greatly depending on the sun's sunspot cycles (it is solar radiation which "ionizes" the ionosphere in the first place). They had already found the shortwave signals to be more reliable in the lulls in between the solar activity associated with peak sunspot years.

The more active the sun's sunspot cycle, the more the magnetic field of the sun interfered with the shortwave radio transmissions. Upon beginning his study, Nelson soon found that the radio interference rose and fell not only with the sunspot cycle, but also with the *motions* of the major planets of the solar system. He discovered that the relative positions of the so-called gas giant planets (Jupiter, Saturn, Uranus and Neptune) along their orbital paths seemed to have the most dramatic effect on the signals:

> It is worthy of note that in 1948, when Jupiter and Saturn were spaced by 120°, and solar activity was at a maximum, radio signals averaged of far higher quality for the year than in 1951 with Jupiter and Saturn at 180° and a considerable decline in solar activity. In other words, the average quality curve of radio signals followed the cycle curve between Jupiter and Saturn rather than the sunspot curve...

So what Nelson concluded is that while the sunspot activity of the sun did have an effect on the quality of shortwave radio signals, the locations of the planets along their orbital paths (especially the major gas giant planets) had a *far greater* effect on the signals. Now, that may not really bother you too much, but the fact is there is nothing—nothing!—in any of the conventional mainstream physics theories which can account for this. Not gravity, not magnetism, nothing. The gravitational influence of these planets is negligible because of their great distance from the Earth and sun. While Jupiter, Saturn, Uranus and Neptune are certainly massive, and we know that the more mass an object has the greater its gravitational field, they are so far away that their influence amounts to virtually nothing. And while magnetic fields like the one the sun generates demonstrably do have an influence on the Earth's ionosphere and hence the quality of the radio signals (which the RCA study proved), the magnetic fields of the distant gas giant planets are far too weak to have an effect, especially an effect that is actually greater than the sun's much more powerful (and much closer) magnetic field. The only conclusion then is that some how, some way, the planets were affecting the quality of radio wave signals on Earth from great distances, and by some means that was as yet undiscovered.

The questions which no one in the mainstream physics community could answer at the time (and they still can't) are exactly what that Force might be, and how it might propagate through the vacuum of space to create the sunspots and the subsequent magnetic activity. Once gravity and magnetism are eliminated, what's left? Well, pretty much nothing, at least in the conventional models—except electricity. We can rule electricity out though because it can't travel through the vacuum of space without a conductor like an electromagnetic plasma, which is a very rare phenomenon. So in the absence of any other plausible explanation, we are left with only one way the Force energy could have traveled the distance between the sun and the outer planets and caused the increased magnetic storms; (you guessed it)...

Higher dimensions.

In the hyperdimensional model of reality, such instantaneous interactions at a distance are not only implied, they are built in to the whole concept. If all you have to do to generate energy is to rotate something, then that means that everything is putting out energy; plants, trees, animals rocks, people—even (and especially) whole planets. As we look at these four gas giant planets (again, Jupiter, Saturn, Uranus and Neptune) we find that they do indeed put out more energy than all the other planets combined. It's just not a kind of energy that modern physicists and astronomers recognize.

The sun holds 99% of the mass in the solar system. If the currently accepted "Laws of Physics" were correct, then that means that the sun must also be the most influential body in the solar system, because it therefore has the most gravity and electromagnetic energy. But if that assumption were correct, then Nelson's RCA experiments would have concluded that the sun's magnetic activity had the greatest influence on the radio signals. Instead, it showed that the *planets* somehow had more influence, which is exactly what we would expect in the hyperdimensional model of reality. Exactly how they do this is through something I've talked about before in my other books like *The Choice*; a source of energy called "angular momentum," or spin energy.

Jupiter, as it turns out, has less than 1% of the mass in the solar system, yet somehow possesses about 60% of the angular momentum. But the sun, which possesses 99% of the mass, has only about 1% of the angular momentum. In fact, as you look at Jupiter, Saturn, Uranus and Neptune, these four planets between them hold more than 98% of the angular momentum in the entire solar system. This is obviously a result of them having been "birthed" by the sun in the solar fission process that Dr. Thomas Van Flandern advocated.

As the sun gave birth to all the planets, like a great cosmic mother, she also gave away most of her own spin energy to them.

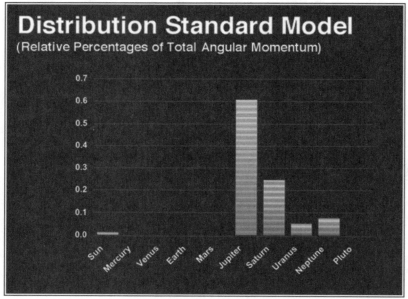

Angular momentum distribution.

The biggest ones (the gas giants) got the most, the smaller terrestrial planets like Earth got a bit less, and in the end this process allowed her to calm herself, spin less intensely, fire off fewer deadly solar flares, burn in a calmer and more consistent way, and create the "habitable zone," a place where higher forms of life like ours could live and flourish. It truly is a beautiful, harmonic and balanced view of how things came to be, almost poetic in its perfection and elegance.

So I ask you here, which view makes more sense? The idea that the sun gave birth to all that we see and experience, at least here in our little corner of the universe, or that it all came together randomly, as the accretion model suggests? For me, I choose the beauty. I choose the idea that we are all part of very big and very beautiful solar family.

OK, back to physics...

Interestingly, these four planets also are unique in another interesting way that relates to the notion that spin energy equates to other types of energy, like heat. Jupiter, Saturn, Neptune and Uranus are the only planets in the solar system that are somehow radiating more heat energy out then they are receiving in from the sun. Somehow, they are behaving like mini stars, and putting out energy which cannot be accounted for in any conventional models.

Now, in those same conventional physics models, spin energy doesn't amount to anything, at least in terms of how the planets might interact with each other. But as we learned earlier, it is spin which creates a portal, or a gateway or a star-gate, whatever you want to call it—through which energy enters our universe. To me it is no surprise then that Nelson found that the four planets with the most spin energy had the greatest physical influence on the sun. But the implications of Nelson's work go way beyond that.

In 2008, the Astronomical Society of Australia published a paper by three astronomers titled "Does a Spin–Orbit Coupling Between the sun and the Jovian Planets Govern the Solar Cycle?" The paper claimed that they had found a link between the rotation of the equatorial region of the sun and the sun's orbital rotation around the barycenter of the solar system (think of it as the center of gravity). They went on to state, "this synchronization is indicative of a spin–orbit coupling mechanism operating between the Jovian planets and the sun." In plain English that means that there was some kind of synchronization or symbiotic relationship between the sun, Jupiter and Saturn that was actually driving the sunspot cycles. Now again, there is absolutely nothing in the conventional view of physics that can account for such a relationship. They even acknowledge as much in in the abstract (summary) of their paper: "However, we are unable to suggest a plausible underlying physical cause for the coupling…"

So this goes even beyond what Nelson found, that the planets had simply an influence on physical reality here on Earth. What the Australian paper shows is that conventional physics has it upside down; the sun doesn't rule the roost because of its size, gravitational and magnetic influences, the planets are the dominant force in our solar system, because they possess almost all the (hyperdimensional) spin energy.

To put it simply, the tail wags the dog, not the other way around. It is spin energy that matters the most, not gravity. Not only that, but the planets and the sun are somehow linked by an unseen Force that somehow propagates through the emptiness of space without being detected. We already know of course how the unseen force propagates; it passes through the higher dimensional aether. This makes it appear as though you can have a cause in one place and an effect in another at the same time. Again, this gives the illusion that the unseen force is traversing the vast three-dimensional distances faster than the speed of light when in fact it isn't. What's instead happening is that the disturbance is caused by something changing here in three dimensions, say Jupiter moving into a 120 degree alignment with the sun. This causes ripples or waves in the aether, the higher dimensions, and just like the ripples on a pond, this wave passes through the higher realms and touches the sun in its higher state. The sun then reacts in some way, perhaps by spitting out a moderately sized solar flare, and the cause and effect appear to be simultaneous because the "wave" or ripple did not visibly travel the distance in between. So while nothing may travel faster than light in 3D, there is no reason it can't do so in the fourth dimension (or higher).

What was even more interesting about Nelson's studies (and other, later studies) was not just that they showed the planets had an influence on the energetic output of the sun; it was the specific geometric configurations under which they did so. A 1951 article in *Time* magazine described them like this:

> Nelson studied the records of RCA's receiving station at Riverhead, N.Y., looking for some correlation between the magnetic storms and the positions of the planets. He found that most of the storms took place when two or more planets were in what he calls a "configuration": i.e., with angles of 0°, 90°, or 180° between the lines connecting them with the sun. The more planets involved in a configuration, the more serious the storm is likely to be. During the great magnetic storm of July 1946, for instance, three planets (the earth, Jupiter and Saturn) were in a configuration, and three others (Mercury, Venus and Mars) were also in a "critical relationship."

One of the things that immediately caught my eye was the fact that these configurations, as Nelson called them, equated with what are known as "specific aspects" in astrology. For instance, when two planets were either lined up with the sun but separated by 180 degrees (which is called an "opposition" in astrology) or at a 90-degree angle to each other (which is called a "square"), there would be heavy magnetic disturbances and storms. Conversely, when the planets were at 120 degrees to each other (called a trine) or at 60 degrees relative to each other (a sextile), the sun was noticeably less active. Using this system, Nelson declared that he could predict the disturbances on the sun with an accuracy of over 90 percent.

Now what's interesting is just what these various "aspects" are said to represent in astrology.

An "opposition" is exactly that. It indicates two or more planets directly opposite each other in the sky (from the viewer's perspective), and it is considered a "tense" aspect, meaning it causes outright conflict between the two planets involved. A square is similar, but not as powerful because the direct opposition has now become a 90-degree alignment. This is also a tense aspect, more akin to friction between the two planets (and what they symbolically represent) rather than outright conflict. The other two configurations, the trine (120 degrees apart on the chart) and the sextile (60 degrees), are harmonious aspects, where everything should flow smoothly and everything should be quiet and peaceful.

So what Nelson found was that these astronomical conditions, two planets at angles of 90 or 180 degrees from each other as an example, exactly correlated to their astrological meanings. Squares and oppositions caused big magnetic storms on the sun, trines and sextiles made the sun quiet. I find the implications of this staggering.

What it means is that not only is astrology real—its longtime assumptions can be correlated in the physical—it is also driven by the astronomy. As the planets move in their orbits about the sun, the changing geometric configurations and alignments change physical conditions in other locations around the solar system. So not only are the laws of physics not laws at all—they can be changed by the whims (and the orbits) of the planets—but they are a local phenomenon. Just as Tip O'Neill (former Speaker of the United States House of Representatives) once quipped "all politics is local," what Nelson and hyperdimensional physics show is that all physics is local too. While the effects may be subtle, the reality is the laws of physics themselves, things like the passage of time and the speed of light, should be different in every different solar system, because they will all have different mixtures of planets, stars, orbital relationships and spin energy.

And there is another implication here that we have to address at this point. Remember, the whole notion of astrology is based on the idea that the planets influence not just our physical reality, but our actual consciousness; that they somehow drive our lives in certain directions and place options and opportunities in our path for us to choose our own destiny. What Nelson's study proved was exactly that; the planets do influence our lives, experiences, emotional states and perhaps even our destinies.

The human brain is nothing but a complex electrical signal transmitter, which is far faster and more complex than any computer. Our brains transmit signals to our bodies, but they also send out (and receive) transmissions in the form of brain waves. The simple truth is that there is really no difference between

Nelson's shortwave radio signals and the neurological signals in your brain, which you experience as thoughts and emotional states. Radio signals are a wave, and your thoughts and feelings are waves as well.

But the point is, if radio waves can be affected by these planetary transitions and movements, our brain waves can too. After all, they are simply different types of electromagnetic transmissions, and theoretically equally vulnerable to being influenced by the planets.

Doesn't it also follow then that astrology, so readily dismissed as a pseudoscience by the scientific community, might have some basis in reality? And even more than that, doesn't it even act as a proof that we all have souls, or higher selves? After all, if everything in the universe is generating energy, and every bit of energy is actually coming from higher dimensions, then aren't our thoughts, which are also nothing more than electrical energy, actually coming from higher dimensions, higher planes?

Without realizing it, Nelson had stumbled upon the key to unlocking some of the deepest mysteries of life. His studies could and did form the basis for proving experimentally, by observation, testing, logic and deduction, that we all are linked to our higher dimensional selves through the aether. And more than that, he provided a basis for us to understand just why we do the things we do, why at certain times in our lives things seem to flow more easily for us, and why at others they seem to pile up and make our lives more difficult.

Another key observation Hoagland and Torun made in these early days was the role that this theorized "tetrahedral physics" might play in another ongoing mystery of the outer solar system.

Beginning in the mid-1960s, ground-based telescopic observations of the solar system began to turn up the startling detection of anomalous internal infrared radiation coming from the planet Jupiter. Later *Pioneer* and *Voyager* spacecraft observations across the 1970s and 80s added the other "gas giant planets," Saturn, Uranus and Neptune, to the list of solar system worlds that somehow, without internal nuclear fusion processes (like stars) still managed to radiate more energy out into space than they receive directly from the sun.

After much initial debate, the conventional understanding of these anomalous "infrared excesses" eventually settled on three possible internal sources:

1. Primordial Heat. Leftover "fossilized thermal echoes" from the enormous energy associated with the accretion and collapse of the planet during its formation. Under this scenario, this energy was still stored inside the planet after literally *billions* of years, but ever more slowly being radiated into space.
2. The Helium Drip Model. Heating caused by eventual internal separation of light elements in gas giant planets (helium from hydrogen), releasing potential energy as the helium falls further toward the center of the planet (a form of ultra-slow, continued gravitational contraction).
3. Radioactive Decay. Anomalous energy release due to excess radioactive decay of heavy element concentrations located within massive gas giant "rocky cores."

Of the three conventional explanations for these "energy anomalies," only the first applies to Jupiter. Because of its mass (318 "Earths"), Jupiter just barely falls into a category of worlds that could retain such primordial heating for the lifetime of the solar system (almost five billion years) and still be able to radiate observable heat.

But when scientists got around to actually measuring the amount of excess heat Jupiter radiates, it quickly became obvious that the "primordial heat model" was inadequate to account for Jupiter's infrared emissions. Even today, the current ratio of absorbed solar energy to emitted (five billion-year-old) internal Jovian energy is still almost *two to one*. This is far in excess of what would be expected after such an enormous amount of time.

After the *Voyager* fly-bys of the 1980s, the second "internal heat" proposal—the "helium drip model"—was favored for the heat excess observed from Saturn. But, because of their relatively light masses (less than thirty times the Earth's), only the third possibility—massive internal radioactive decay—has been seriously attempted as an explanation for Uranus' and Neptune's more puzzling anomalous infrared emissions. There are, however, serious problems with all of these conventional explanations for all planets less massive than Jupiter.

During the *Voyager* encounters of Uranus and Neptune, spacecraft instruments detected a barely measurable (but significant) "infrared excess" for Uranus of about 1.14 to 1. Whereas for Neptune, essentially Uranus' planetary "twin," the ratio of internal heat to intercepted sunlight was a striking *three to one.*

However, simultaneous Doppler tracking gravity measurements conducted during the fly-bys detected no anomalous central concentrations of heavy elements in either planet. This would be *required* if the excess observed IR radiation is, in fact, caused by excessive internal radioactive element concentrations.

Having failed to confirm the radioactive decay model, the conventional planetary physicists began to search around for an alternative explanation for Uranus' excess energy output. They quickly seized on the one characteristic that separates Uranus from all other bodies in the solar system—its pronounced "axial tilt."

Compared to all the other planets of the solar system Uranus has an "obliquity" (the technical term) some 98° to the plane of its orbit of the sun; Neptune's is much more "normal": about 30°. (In comparison, Earth's obliquity is about 23.5°.) This led to a new proposal, the "recent collision model." This asserted that Uranus—somehow, long after its formation—suffered a massive impact with another major object, perhaps an errant moon. This, according to the theorists, in addition to accounting for the current "tipped over situation" of the planet, would have also added a significant amount of geologically "recent" internal energy to Uranus, driving up internal temperatures by equivalent amounts. This model argues that these resulting elevated temperatures in Uranus, derived from a massive cosmic collision, could thus account for Uranus' current infrared excess, as observed by *Voyager* in 1986.

Unfortunately, this explanation also quickly ran into difficulties. For one thing, Uranus is barely radiating "over unity" (more energy coming out than is going in) at its distance from the sun, while Neptune is radiating almost three times more energy "out" than it's getting from the sun. When these two planets are "normalized" (i.e., when their differing distances from the sun are

139

taken into account), their *absolute* internal "over unity" energy emissions are, in fact, just about the same. If the recent collision model was correct, Uranus should be radiating far more than Neptune. In fact, there is virtually no difference. If a moon or other large object had recently struck Uranus, it certainly was not responsible for the planet's excess heat emissions.

What Hoagland then began to consider was that there might be an *external* source for this anomalous heat output, perhaps the same source that was fueling the 19.5° upwellings—but what could be the source of this mysterious excess energy that seemed to defy conventional explanation and conform to occult geometric rules?

At this point, Hoagland and Torun had a conundrum. They had certainly developed a series of observations and connections that demanded closer scrutiny—but in what context? It was not enough to argue that the Cydonia ruins imparted knowledge of tetrahedral geometry and that this geometry seemed to have some reflected physical effects in the rotating bodies of the solar system. They had to have a coherent model of the *mechanism* that was driving all of these observed planetary upwellings and the anomalous heat output. The pattern itself implied that there was an underlying physics involving the energy upwellings.

There is a perfectly natural explanation for such "anomalous energy" appearing in celestial bodies—unfortunately, it hasn't been seriously considered by science for over a hundred years. Hoagland found that the idea that "forces"—like gravity or magnetism—could be modeled geometrically was becoming quite popular within modern mathematics. With that in mind, he began to look back at physics theories from the 1800s, and found that the very father of modern-day physics, James Clerk Maxwell, had indeed dabbled in some equations that seemed to fit what he and Torun had observed on the outer planets. Maxwell had routinely argued that the only way to solve certain problems in physics was to account for some phenomena as 3D "reflections" of objects existing in higher spatial dimensions. When Maxwell died, this higher dimensional or "scalar" component was stripped out of his equations by Oliver Heaviside, and the resulting "classic Maxwell equations" became the basis for our modern-day models of electromagnetic force. But if Maxwell's original work was correct—even though it had been discarded—then that meant his original concepts could potentially explain the various planetary phenomena Hoagland and Torun had observed. Tentatively, Hoagland began to examine more closely this early model of "hyperdimensional physics."

Hoagland found that a number of modern-day mathematicians had actually begun to model these possible higher dimensions geometrically. "Topologists" like H. S. M. Coxeter had done a significant amount of work in mapping the higher dimensional properties of a rotating "hypersphere," a sphere that exists in more than just three spatial dimensions. As noted above, the mathematics describing this "hypersphere," and the multiple dimensions above it, are extremely arcane. Yet the *signatures* of this higher dimensional physics—as reflected in our own 3D universe—are much easier to spot and predict. His equations predicted that such a figure—if it was *rotated*—would create roiling vorticular motions (exactly like the observed dynamics of Jupiter's "Great Red Spot") in the sphere's 3D geometry, and at the *specific* latitude—19.5°.

This was exactly what Hoagland and Torun were seeing in their own observations of the rotating planets and moons of the solar system. If these observations were indeed linked to the higher dimensional properties of the "rotating hypersphere," then it meant not only that rotating *planets* existed simultaneously in multiple, higher spatial dimensions, but also that this new physics could provide potentially limitless amounts of energy to drive the observed dynamics of their atmospheres, their internal fluid motions, their surface geological "upwellings"—everything! Even, ultimately, "life" itself.

To recap concepts we have previously introduced, the cornerstone of the hyperdimensional model is the notion that "higher" spatial dimensions not only exist, but are also the underlying foundation upon which our entire 3D reality exists. Beyond that, everything in our observable 3D world is, in fact, driven by mathematically modeled "information transfer" from these higher dimensions. This "information transfer" might simply be the result of changes in the geometry of a connected system, say a change in the orbital parameters of a planet, like Jupiter or the

Earth. Since we are limited in our perceptions to the 3D universe we live in, we cannot "see" these higher dimensions. However, we can see (and measure) *changes* in these higher dimensions that have *simultaneous* effect on *our* reality. By definition, this change in higher dimensional geometry is perceived in our 3D universe as an "energy output"—like the various 19.5° planetary energy upwellings we have noted previously.

The hyperdimensional model therefore implicitly argues that, contrary to Einstein's dictates, instantaneous "action at a distance" in our universe is indeed possible—in fact, it is a given—because of this higher dimensional information transfer. The model predicts that the effects of a "cause" in our three dimensions, whatever it may be, can be felt in measurable and predictable ways in our perceived universe at speeds incomparably greater than that of light. The universe accomplishes this seemingly impossible feat by the transformation and transfer of information (as a different "energy") through "hyperspace," i.e., through these higher spatial dimensions. In our familiar three dimensions, this information/ energy is then transformed back into familiar energy forms, like light, heat and even gravity itself.

Changes in one gravitationally-connected system on a large scale, like the planetary scale of a solar system, can therefore have an instantaneous, measurable effect on other bodies in the same system—providing there is a "resonance condition" (a "matched" connection) between those two objects via hyperspace. Thus, the hyperdimensional model argues that everything, even widely separated three-space objects like remote planets, are ultimately connected through this four-space interaction; meaning that a "cause" in one place (like Jupiter) can have an "effect" in another (like the sun)—without any measurable 3D force (such as an electromagnetic wave) having measurably traversed the three-space distance *in between*.

Mainstream physics teaches us that this phenomenon— called "non-locality," which has been observed for decades in laboratory experiments[1] is simply a baffling "quantum reality" limited to ultra-short distances at the subatomic level, but that it does not, and *cannot*, affect larger objects at great distances (like planets, stars or galaxies themselves). Because the speed of light is theorized to be the absolute speed limit of our 3D macro-universe, no cause is supposed to have a measurable effect on any object anywhere sooner than it takes light to travel the distance in between. Yet these "magical," faster-than-light signals between atomic particles, and even communication between photons, has now been overwhelmingly confirmed at macro distances as well. Our current understanding of the limiting speed of light, based on Maxwell's equations of electromagnetism, asserts that only certain kinds of energy, like electromagnetic radiation, can even travel long distances through the vacuum of space.

In this classical "Einsteinian" view of physics, there is no "aether"—as it was called in Maxwell's day—to carry electromagnetic radiation's transverse waves across the vacuum. In the hyperdimensional model, the aether is *back*—as the actual transformation medium between the higher spatial realities and *our* dimension—through something called the "torsion field" (the word "torsion" is formed from the same root as "torque," and means "to spin").

So a torsion field is a *"spin* field"—a crucial point we will come back to later.

The torsional-aetheric field is, therefore, *not* the 19th century's "electromagnetic aether" at all—but rather a spin-sensitive, geometric aetheric *state*—whereby hyperdimensional information/energy *is* detectable in our dimension via spinning vorticular (rotating and/or precessing) physical systems.

Contrary to mainstream physics dogma, a rich series of experiments—for over a hundred years—have overwhelmingly confirmed various aspects of this *non-electromagnetic* "spin-field aether." The still-developing mathematics and graphs that model this theoretical cosmology now, unfortunately, are as Byzantine and arcane as anything in science today. However, this mathematics is reinforced by a veritable explosion of theoretical papers and fascinating laboratory experiments which have been secretly carried out in Russia for over 50 years—only becoming widely available here (via the Internet) with the collapse of the Soviet Empire.

So even though there is substantial and growing reason to suspect that the hyperdimensional/torsion model may ultimately be correct as the "Theory of Everything," most modern physicists (certainly in the West) still reject the notion, and stubbornly don't want to "go there."

Yet that was not always the prevailing sentiment in Western physics.

The mathematical and physical parameters required for such "information/energy gating" into this spatial dimension from potential "*n*-dimensions" were primarily founded in the work of several nineteenth century founders of modern mathematics and physics. Among these were German mathematician Georg Riemann; Scottish physicist Sir William Thompson (who would eventually be knighted by the British crown as "Baron Kelvin of Largs" for his scientific and technological contributions); Scottish physicist James Clerk Maxwell; and British mathematician Sir William Rowan Hamilton.

Riemann mathematically initiated the nineteenth century scientific community (if not the rest of Victorian society) into the unsettling idea of "hyperspace" on June 10, 1854. In a seminal presentation made at the University of Göttingen in Germany, Riemann put forth the first mathematical description of the possibility of "higher, unseen dimensions" under the deceptively simple title "On the Hypotheses Which Lie at the Foundation of Geometry."

Reimann's paper was a fundamental assault on the two-thousand-year-old assumptions of "Euclidian geometry"—the ordered, rectilinear laws of "ordinary" 3D reality. In its place, Reimann proposed a *4D* reality (of which our 3D reality was merely a "subset"), in which the geometric rules were radically different, but also internally self-consistent. Even more radically, Reimann proposed that the basic laws of nature in three-space, the three mysterious forces then known to physics—electrostatics, magnetism and gravity—were all fundamentally *united* in four-space, and merely "looked different" because of the resulting "crumpled geometry" of our 3D reality. In essence, he argued that gravity, magnetism and electricity were all the same thing—energies coming from higher dimensions.

Reimann was suggesting a major break with Newton's "force creates action-at-a-distance" theories. These had been proposed to explain the "magical" properties of magnetic and electrical attraction and repulsion, gravitationally curved motions of planets and falling apples for over 200 years. In place of Newton, Reimann was proposing that such "apparent forces" are a direct result of objects moving through three-space geometry, *distorted* by the intruding geometry of four-space.

It is clear that Maxwell and other "giants" of nineteenth century physics (Kelvin, for one), as well as an entire contemporary generation of mathematicians (like Cayle, Tait, etc.), took Reimann's ideas very much to heart; Maxwell's original selection of four-space "quaternions" as the mathematical operators for his force equations and descriptions of electrical and magnetic interaction, clearly demonstrate his belief in Reimann's approach—as does his surprising literary excursions into poetry, vividly extolling the implications of "higher-dimensional realities," including musings on their relationship to the ultimate origin of the human soul... emphatically confirming this same outlook.[2]

In 1867, following decades of inquiry into the fundamental properties of both matter and the space between, Thompson proposed a radical new explanation for the most fundamental properties of solid objects: the existence of "the vortex atom." This was in direct contradiction to then-prevailing theories of matter, in which atoms were still viewed as infinitesimally "small, hard bodies [as] imagined by [the Roman poet] Lucretius, and endorsed by Newton..." Thompson's "vortex atoms" were envisioned, instead, as tiny, self-sustaining "whirlpools" in the so-called "aether"—which Thompson and his contemporaries increasingly believed extended throughout the universe as an all-pervasive, incompressible fluid.

Even as Thompson published his revolutionary model for the atom, Maxwell, building on Thompson's earlier explorations of the underlying properties of this "aetheric fluid," was well on the way to devising a highly successful "mechanical" vortex model of the "incompressible aether" itself, in which Thompson's vortex atom could live—a model derived in part from the laboratory-observed elastic and dynamical properties of solids. Ultimately, in 1873, he would succeed in uniting a couple hundred years' worth of electrical and magnetic scientific observations into a

145

comprehensive, overarching electromagnetic theory of light vibrations, carried across space by this "incompressible and highly stressed universal aetheric fluid."

Maxwell's mathematical basis for his triumphant unification of these two great mystery forces of nineteenth century physics were "quaternions," a term invented (adopted would be a more precise description) in the 1840s by mathematician Sir William Rowan Hamilton, for "an ordered *pair* of complex numbers." Complex numbers themselves, according to Hamilton, were nothing more than "pairs of real numbers which are added or multiplied according to certain formal rules." In 1897, A. S. Hathaway formally extended Hamilton's ideas regarding quaternions as "sets of four real numbers" to the idea of *four spatial dimensions*, in a paper entitled "Quaternions as Numbers of Four-Dimensional Space."[3]

According to Maxwell, action at a distance *was* possible through the "aether," which he defined as higher spatial dimensions—or what we now call "hyperspace." In other words, the father of modern terrestrial electromagnetic physics had come to the same conclusions as Hoagland's theorized "Martian architect" at Cydonia.

This may seem to be a tenuous connection at first, but when you read certain lines from his poem presented to the Committee of the Cayley Portrait Fund in 1887, it becomes quite clear, that he *knew*:

"Ye cubic surfaces! By threes and nines, draw round his camp your seven-and-twenty lines—the *Seal of Solomon in three dimensions*..."

This clear description of the "Seal of Solomon in three dimensions," is an overt reference to the geometrical and mathematical underpinnings of the infamous "circumscribed tetrahedral geometry" memorialized all over Cydonia. If you take the base figure of a tetrahedron—the equilateral triangle—and add a second equilateral triangle to the figure exactly opposite the first, and then circumscribe that figure with a circle, you get the familiar "Star of David," the "Seal of Solomon" that Maxwell describes. And in this figure, the tips of the double triangle touch the circle at the poles and at 19.5° north and south, directly linking the

A three-dimensional Seal of Solomon.

identical, *hyperdimensional quaternion geometry* whose physical effects we have now rediscovered all across the solar system. And, of course, taking this "Seal of Solomon" and drawing it in three dimensions would give you a double-star tetrahedron circumscribed by a sphere. The reference to "seven and twenty lines" is also a not-so-subtle reference to a 2D sketch of a double tetrahedron encompassed by a "hypercube," shown as a base 2D form of a hexagon.

In a tragedy for science, two other 19th century "mathematical physicists"—Oliver Heaviside and William Gibbs—"streamlined" Maxwell's original equations down to four simple (if woefully incomplete) expressions after Maxwell's death. Because Heaviside openly felt the quaternions were "an abomination"—never fully understanding the linkage between the critical scalar (a directionless measurement, like speed) and vector (a directionally defined value, like displacement) components in Maxwell's use of them to describe the energy potentials of empty space ("apples and oranges," he termed them)—he eliminated over *twenty quaternions* from Maxwell's original theory in his attempted "simplification."

Oliver Heaviside was once described (by *Scientific American*) as "self-taught and... never connected with any university... [he] had [however] a remarkable and inexplicable ability to arrive

147

at mathematical results of considerable complexity without going through any conscious process of proof." According to other observers, Heaviside actually felt that Maxwell's use of quaternions and their description of the "potentials" of space was "mystical, and should be murdered from the theory." By drastically editing Maxwell's original work after the latter's death, excising the scalar component of the quaternions and eliminating the hyperspatial characteristics of the directional (vector) component, he effectively accomplished this goal single-handedly.[4]

This means, of course, that the four surviving classic "Maxwell equations"—which appear in every electrical and physics text the world over, as *the* underpinnings of *all* twentieth century electrical and electromagnetic engineering—never appeared in *any* original Maxwell paper or treatise. And every invention, from radio to radar, from television to computer science to every "hard" science from physics to chemistry to astrophysics that deals with these electromagnetic radiative processes, are based on these supposed "Maxwell equations."

They are, in fact, *Heaviside's* equations, *not* Maxwell's. The end result was that physics lost its promising theoretical beginnings as a truly "hyperdimensional" science over a century ago, and instead was saddled with a very limited subset of that potentially unifying theory, thanks to Heaviside.

The advocates of an aether-based model of force were dealt a greater blow in 1887, when the Michelson-Morley experiments effectively proved there was "no material aether." What was lost, however, because of Heaviside, was that Maxwell had never believed in a material aether himself—he was assuming a *hyperspatial* aether simultaneously connecting everything in the universe.

The major source of confusion surrounding Maxwell's actual theory, versus what Heaviside reduced it to, is its math—a notation system perhaps best described by H. J. Josephs:

> Hamilton's algebra of quaternions, unlike Heaviside's algebra of vectors, is not a mere abbreviated mode of expressing Cartesian analysis, but is an independent branch of mathematics with its own rules of operation and its own

special theorems. A quaternion is, in fact, a generalized or hypercomplex number.

In 1897, Hathaway published a paper specifically identifying these hypercomplex numbers as "numbers in four-dimensional space." Thus, modern physics' apparent ignorance of Maxwell's nineteenth century success—a mathematically based, 4D "field-theory"—would seem to originate from a basic lack of knowledge of the true nature of Hamilton's quaternion algebra itself.

And, unless you track down an original 1873 copy of Maxwell's "Treatise," there is no easy way to verify the existence of Maxwell's "hyperdimensional" quaternion notation; for, by 1892, the third edition incorporated a "correction" to Maxwell's original use of "scalar potentials," thus removing a crucial distinction between four-space "geometric potential," and a three-space "vector field" from all subsequent Maxwellian theory—which is why modern physicists apparently don't realize that Maxwell's original equations *were*, in fact, the first geometric four-space field theory, expressed in specific four-space terms—the language of quaternions.

As Hoagland continued to make new connections of the geometry of Cydonia with the historical treatment of hyperspatial realities, he encountered a number of independent, rogue experimentalists who had been working along these same lines. Foremost among these were Dr. Bruce DePalma, an M.I.T. physicist and researcher, and Lt. Col. Thomas Bearden, a nuclear engineer and physicist who had been working on Maxwell's original model since his days on the US Army's scalar weapons programs.

Bearden had tirelessly researched Maxwell's original writings, and concluded that Maxwell's original theory is, in fact, the Holy Grail of physics—the first successful unified field theory in the history of science. Bearden had done dogged detective work to uncover Maxwell's papers, and from them had concluded that Heaviside had literally hijacked Maxwell's theory and set modern science back almost a hundred years. According to Bearden, not only would modern physics *never* find the single unifying element for gravity, electricity and magnetism (because it was all based on

Heaviside's broken version of Maxwell's model), but that if the original model were restored, it had the potential to unleash nearly limitless amounts of energy, and to allow humanity the means to actually "engineer" forces like gravity at the quantum level.

This radical view was supported by Bearden's own research, which was based on papers and experiments carried out by Sir Edmund Whittaker and Nikola Tesla in the early twentieth century, and later confirmed in the so-called "Aharonov-Bohm" experiments.[5]

Tesla, the inventor of modern civilization (through his discovery of alternating current), had conducted a number of relevant experiments in his lab in Colorado Springs in 1899. During one experiment, he observed and recorded "interfering scalar waves." Via massive experimental radio transmitters he had built on a mountaintop in Colorado, he was broadcasting and receiving (by his own assertion) longitudinal stresses (as opposed to conventional EM "transverse waves") through the vacuum. This he was accomplishing with his own, hand-engineered equipment (produced according to Maxwell's original, quaternion equations), when he detected an interference "return" from a passing line of thunderstorms. Tesla termed the phenomenon a "standing columnar wave," and tracked it electromagnetically for hours as the cold front moved across the west. Tesla's experiments were suddenly stopped when his benefactor, J. P. Morgan, discovered the true purpose of his experiment—to generate unlimited amounts of electricity "too inexpensive to charge for."

Bearden was also interested in generating energy by creating "longitudinal stress" in the vacuum using Maxwell's quaternion/hyperdimensional potentials. Bearden wrote several papers on the theory, eventually published by the Department of Energy on their official web site.[6]

Bearden then set about the task of actually constructing a device that could draw "energy from the vacuum," eventually patenting a device (The "Motionless Electromagnetic Generator") that seems to generate energy from literally *nothing*.[7]

Of course, you can't really get something from nothing, and Hoagland quickly realized that the effect Bearden was describing was the same "hyperdimensional" effect he was seeing in the heat generation of the outer planets.

There is now much fevered discussion among Western physicists on the Quantum Electrodynamics Zero Point Energy of space—"the energy of the vacuum." To many familiar with the original works of Maxwell, Kelvin, et. al., this sounds an awful lot like the once-familiar "aether," merely updated and now passing under an assumed name. Described as some sort of exotic quantum effect to make it seem acceptable, this "zero point energy" is nothing more than Maxwell's hyperdimensional physics in another guise.

Thus, creating and then relieving a "stress" in Maxwell's vorticular aether is precisely equivalent to tapping the energy of the vacuum that, according to current quantum mechanics models, possesses a staggering amount of such energy per cubic inch of empty space. Even inefficiently releasing a tiny percentage of this "strain energy" into our three dimensions, or into a body existing in 3D space, could make it appear as if the energy was coming from nowhere—something from nothing. In other words, to an entire generation of students and astrophysicists woefully ignorant of Maxwell's original equations, such energy would appear as the dreaded "P" word… "perpetual motion."

As we shall show, it is this "new" source of energy—in a far more controlled context—that seems to also be responsible for not only the anomalous infrared excesses Hoagland has noted in the so-called giant outer planets of this solar system, but for the radiated energies of stars themselves.

Yet how does one create a "stress in the aether" to generate energy, or test this hyperdimensional physics theory? The theoretical notions of Maxwell and Bearden had already been tested, albeit inadvertently, by the aforementioned Dr. DePalma.

DePalma, brother of the famed film director Brian DePalma, long before he and Hoagland met, had been running (since the 70s) a series of groundbreaking "rotational experiments" which remarkably confirmed much of what Hoagland would be theoretically rediscovering twenty years later! One practical invention was DePalma's famous "N-Machine"—a high-speed, "homopolar generator" which is able to pull measurable electrical power literally out of "thin air" (the vacuum) with no expenditure of fuel.

Among DePalma's many other radical results was an experiment in which he simultaneously ejected two metal balls—one spinning at over 27,000 rpm and one not spinning at all—from the same test rig. He then measured the rate at which they both rose and fell. In shocking contrast to the expected result if standard "Newtonian" mechanics are at work, the spinning ball *rose farther and faster, and fell to the ground faster,* than the non-spinning ball—even though exactly the same upward force (momentum) had been applied to both.

The implication was that the *spinning ball* had somehow managed to gain energy from somewhere—which simultaneously altered both the effects of gravity *and* inertia on it—exactly as Bearden's model had independently proposed.

DePalma conducted countless additional rotational experiments, including with massive gyroscopes, throughout the 1970s. In the course of these mechanics, he discovered that gyros, when spun up, and simultaneously induced to mechanically precess (wobble on their axes of rotation), could also be used to substantially negate the effects of gravity. In one experiment, a 276-pound "force machine" was reduced in weight by *six pounds*—about a 2 % loss—when the gyros were switched on.

DePalma also discovered that these massive rotating systems, even when carefully isolated, could induce "anomalous rotational motions" in other gyroscopic setups, even in other rooms, but only if they were *also* rotating.

As a result of these years of painstaking laboratory experimentation, with a great variety of different spinning systems, DePalma ultimately argued that all rotating objects—including planets and stars—*must intrinsically* precess. "Precession" is the tendency of spinning objects, like a child's top or a planet like the Earth, to wobble on their rotational axes. In conventional mechanics, precessional motion is explained as coming from an outside force (like the Moon's gravity tidally tugging on the Earth's slightly bulging equator) unbalancing an object's spin.

Based on DePalma's empirically-derived measurements of rotation, he predicted that even apparently isolated spinning objects would precess—by virtue of their interaction with other rotating

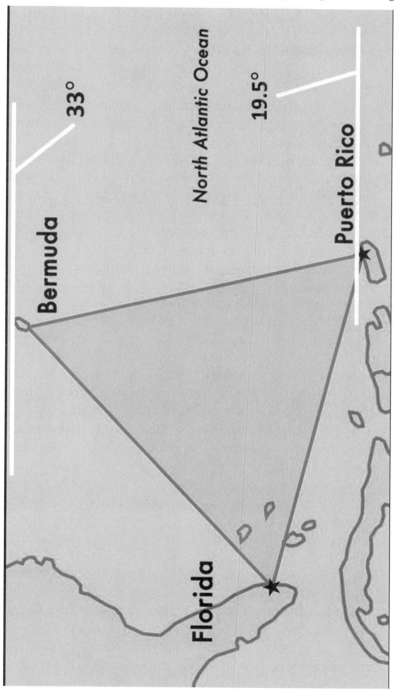

The Triangle, with northern and southern boundaries marked.

objects. They drew energy from some kind of non-magnetic, non-gravitational field (termed "the OD field"), which he proposed had to exist to explain his perplexing "energy accreting" spinning ball experiment. Ironically, totally unknown to DePalma—because of the Cold War and the KGB's strict secrecy controls—what he was observing was also being simultaneously observed by his Russian counterparts, and termed "a torsion field" based on the same *rotational* interactions.

The idea of "isolated precession"—the logical conclusion of DePalma's decades of observations of all kinds of anomalous spinning systems—has never been experimentally examined under controlled laboratory conditions (at least, in any published literature in the West), as DePalma needed a "zero gravity" (force-free) environment to conduct the proper test. Unfortunately, before Hoagland (with his NASA associations and connections) could conclude arrangements for just such test of Bruce's remarkable hypothesis, to be conducted at NASA-Lewis's vacuum zero gravity drop test facility, DePalma suddenly died in 1998.

Ultimately, DePalma's fascinating prediction concerning *intrinsic* rotational precession—which can now be elegantly explained by invoking multiple rotational motions and torsion interactions occurring *simultaneously* in *higher dimensions*—will come to have great significance in our story later on.

With Bearden and DePalma's experimental input in hand, Hoagland began to consider serious methods of doing the one thing that all the other hyperdimensional theories had been unable to accomplish—carry out actual *testing* of their core assumptions.

The true scientific method is something that is woefully misunderstood in our modern world, even by many scientists today. The history of science is replete with debates that have raged back and forth in colossal wars of ego and self-interest—but the method itself is supposed to protect us from scientists becoming a new priesthood, by making sure that when models don't fit the new data, they are discarded, no matter how appealing they may be to some interests. Unfortunately, it rarely works that way.

Hoagland wanted to immediately separate his concept of hyperdimensional physics from the earlier models in one distinct way—prediction. Only if his new ideas could be either confirmed or falsified would his modern version of Maxwell's revolutionary ideas ever gain traction—and in order to accomplish that, the first order of business for any valid scientific model is to produce *testable predictions* based on that model. Fortunately, there were several implicit tests of the hyperdimensional model almost immediately suggested by the original observations themselves. Eventually, Hoagland settled on four additional key predictions that would determine if Cydonia's "embedded tetrahedral physics" and the resulting "hyperdimensional model" would be falsifiable.

At this point, then, *only* the hyperdimensional theory:

1. Points to the deepest implications of the simple astronomical fact that the "tail wags the dog"—that the planets in this physics are fully capable of exerting a determinant influence on the sun, and each other, through their disproportionate ratio of total solar system angular momentum: over 100 to 1, in the (known) planets' favor.

2. Possesses the precise physical mechanism—via Maxwell's "changing quaternion scalar potentials"—accounting for this anomalous planetary angular momentum influence.

3. Has already publicly identified, at the United Nations in 1992, a blatant geometric clue to this entire hyperdimensional solar process: the maximum sunspot numbers (those large, relatively "cool," rotating vortices appearing on the solar surface), rising, falling and methodically changing latitude, during the course of the familiar twenty-two-year solar cycle—and peaking every half-cycle (around eleven years), at the solar latitude of about 19.5°.

Later, it was discovered that there was a coherent mathematical connection between the 19.5 number and the "Masonic" 33 degrees that was always appearing in their symbols and literature. This implies that they understood the mystical/mathematical extradimensional connection between them.

So what, ultimately does this have to do with the Triangle? It honestly wasn't until I realized the locations of Bermuda and Puerto Rico, the northern and southern boundaries of the Triangle were 33° and 19.5° respectively that I figured it out. The Triangle rests exactly inside what is effectively a "hyperdimensional

155

vortex," bordered by these two mystically critical latitudes where the walls between the dimensions are thinnest. It is for that reason I think that so many strange, inexplicable things happen there, and will continue to happen until we realize the real physics operating there, and take steps to warn those that traverse the region.

And it is this physics, the ease with which they can slip back and forth between dimensions or even manipulate wormholes, that attracts the alien presence. Not the other way around.

Next, and finally, we will look at the role this underlying driving may have played in some of the most famous unsolved undersea mysteries and disappearances in the Triangle.

(Endnotes)
1 "An experimental test of non-local realism" by S. Gröblacher et. al., *Nature* 446, 871, April 2007 | "To be or not to be local" by Alain Aspect, *Nature* 446, 866, April 2007
2 "My soul is an entangled knot, Upon a liquid vortex wrought. By Intellect in the Unseen residing. And thine doth like a convict sit, With marlinspike untwisting it, Only to find its knottiness abiding; Since all the tool for its untying."—James Clerk Maxwell, "A Paradoxical Ode."
3 *Bulletin of the American Mathematical Society.* [4 (1887), 54-7]
4 *Bulletin of the Calcutta Mathematical Society*, Vol. 20, 1928-29, p.202. "Oliver Heaviside: Sage in Solitude" (IEEE Press, New York, 1988, p.9, note 3.
5 "On the Partial Differential Equations of Mathematical Physics." (*Mathematische Annalen*, vol. 57, 1903. p. 333-335); "On an Expression of the Electromagnetic Field Due to Electrons by Means of Two Scalar Potential Functions." (*Proceedings of the London Mathematical Society*, vol. 1, 1904. p. 367-372.); Nikola Tesla, Colorado Springs Notes 1899-1900, Nolit, Beograd, Yugoslavia, 1978. p. 61-62.
6 http://www.apfn.org/Free_Energy/electromagnetic.pdf
7 http://jnaudin.free.fr/meg/meg.htm

Chapter 6

Ancient Civilizations and USOs

To this point, we have covered the major mysteries of the Triangle both above the sea and on the sea. But we have paid no attention at all to what may or may not lie in the oceans beneath the Triangle. Certainly, there is ample material to consider, going all the way back to Columbus' sighting of a USO (Unidentified Submerged Object) on his epic voyage to the Americas in 1492. This is especially critical given the working theory that the Triangle is important because of its geographical placement between these now two established critical latitudes: 19.5°N and 33°N, where, as we have seen, the "magic" happens. As you look beneath the sea not just in the area of the Triangle but in fact all long both latitudes, you see an extraordinary number of strange events, deep ocean ruins and, especially, aboveground megalithic monuments.

Foremost among these are locations like the Mayan ruins at Chichen Itza, the pyramid complex at Teotihuacan, and the extraordinary deep sea ruins off the coast of Cuba. At the 33rd parallel we find all manner of interesting megalithic sites, the Chinese pyramid complex of Xi'an, the American cities of Phoenix (founded as a Federal protectorate by 33rd degree Scottish Rite Freemason president Ulysses S. Grant as a Masonic capital) and Atlanta (Atlantis). These certainly imply that the builders of these sites understood the significance of these latitudes and how they played into the occulted energetic grid of the planet itself, which somehow feeds the anomalous weather and incidents we see in the Triangle.

But historically, we also see multiple encounters with deep sea vehicles, what are today referred to as "USOs." There are many

157

types of USOs, ranging from the mysterious subsurface lights Columbus saw to actual reports of flying vehicles emerging out of the sea observed by military and commercial shipping vessels. While I was filming the reality show *Uncovering Aliens* for Discovery back in 2014, I spoke with multiple witnesses who saw glowing green and/or blue orbs of significant size rising from and descending into Lake Michigan on a regular basis for decades, giving rise to the notion that there may have been an underwater base in the lake itself. Rumors have persisted of undersea bases, both human and extraterrestrial, just off Catalina Island in California for decades, along with reports of submerged lights reported by ferries and hydrofoils that take vacationers to the island's primary port of Avalon. Other reports of a secret underground base underneath a shelf off of Malibu remain unsubstantiated and are based on spurious interpretations of Google Earth compression artifacts.

There have always been rumors of UFO encounters at sea, especially military ones, and even though they did not take place in the Triangle, they bear some examination.

One such alleged encounter surfaced (excuse the pun) in 2017 with the leak of photos that include what is undeniably a USO emerging from the ocean near Iceland in 1971. The photos were first seen in a French paranormal magazine called *Top Secret,* and later, similar photos were emailed to UFO researcher Alex Mistretta. Mistretta made them available to the web site Black Vault and researcher John Greenewald, who as I understand it posted them in an article on the Black Vault web site. According to BlackVault. com, the photos show the emergence of a classic USO from the ocean, observed through a periscope; the object performed a series of maneuvers before shooting away into the sky. Allegedly, the photos were taken by the crew of the USS *Trepang* (SSN 674) in March of 1971. The *Trepang*, a Sturgeon class nuclear armed and powered attack submarine, was allegedly commanded by an Admiral Dean R. Sackett and the photographs may have been taken by a Ship's Mate named John Klika. Supposedly, the encounter occurred in the Atlantic between Iceland and a Norwegian island named Jan Mayen, which hosts the Norwegian Meteorological Institute and a Norwegian military base. Using various methods, Mistretta and Greenewald were able to confirm the following

Photo 1 from the USS *Trepang*.

details, which I have also independently confirmed:[1]

    1) The photos were taken from a United States Navy submarine.
    2) The location was between Iceland and Jan Mayen Island in the Atlantic Ocean.
    3) They were taken in March of 1971.
    4) The Submarine was the Navy's USS *Trepang* (SSN

674) and the Admiral on board was Dean Reynolds Sackett.

5) The Submarine came upon the object by "accident," as they were in the region on a routine joint military and scientific expedition. Officer John Klika was the one who initially spotted the object with the periscope.

We know for a fact that the USS *Trepang* existed, that she was in the area between Iceland and Jan Mayen Island in March of 1971, that Admiral Dean Reynolds Sackett was in command, and

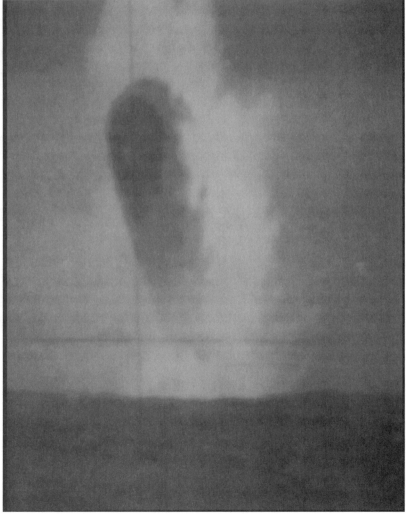

Photo 2 from the USS *Trepang*.

that a "John Klika" was listed as a Ship's Mate in the vessel's duty roster.[2] What we do not know for a fact is whether Klika took the photos in question, whether there was more than one object (there appears to be) or more than one encounter (a possibility). In an effort to follow up, UPARS-LA researcher Steve Murillo was able to track down both Admiral Sackett and Ship's Mate Klika, who both denied seeing anything unusual in the area at the time. Sackett agreed to view the photos, and after viewing them he commented

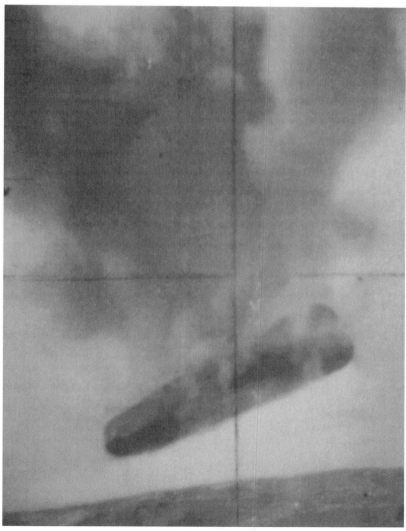

Photo 3 from the USS *Trepang*.

coyly, "All I saw was ice."[1]

Looking at the photographs themselves, at least some of them appear to be authentic and are plausibly from the 1971 time period. They show at least one and possibly two different objects. According to Mistretta's source the *Trepang* encountered the object just after the ship had surfaced after performing a military mission for several weeks under the ice. Klika was claimed to be the officer who initially spotted the object through the periscope. In looking at the first two pictures, they are consistent with those

Photo 4 from the USS *Trepang*.

reports.

Both photos show a large cylindrical object emerging from the sea, apparently at high speed. In both photos the crosshairs of the periscope sight is visible, indicating that, as the story goes, it was taken though the view port. The first image catches the object just as it breaks the plane of the water line, and in the other we can see the spray of the ocean as the object moves upward with what is evidently a considerable degree of momentum. This is entirely consistent with a large, massive object breaking through from

Photo 5 from the USS *Trepang*.

163

below the sea.

In the next photo, the cylindrical object has now broken completely through the surface of the water and starts to rotate horizontally. Water can be seen dripping off the surface of the object and there appears to be a significant amount of dark smoke above and around it. It is unclear if this is some sort of exhaust coming from the object or if it has been fired upon by the ship. In the fourth photo the object has turned and stabilized, water still dripping off it, and it appears to be hovering in a stationary position above the ocean. Once again we see the crosshairs of the

Photo 6 from the USS *Trepang*.

periscope viewfinder and that implies these photos were also taken through the viewfinder.

In the next set of pictures the object begins to rotate, first along the horizontal axis (which reveals a bulging "belly" on the bottom) and then about the center of gravity, where it assumes a more "flying wing" shape. Neither of these photos appears to be taken through the periscope, possibly indicating they are from a

Photo 7 from the USS *Trepang*.

different camera and possibly taken from the deck, conning tower or some other vantage point. There is no sign of crosshairs or other indication they were taken through the periscope. It is also notable that the ocean looks very different from the first four photos with far more reflected sunlight, implying that they are a of a different object, from a different ship, taken at another time of day, or simply the disparities may be due to the use of a different camera and film combination. Truthfully however, they appear to be of a

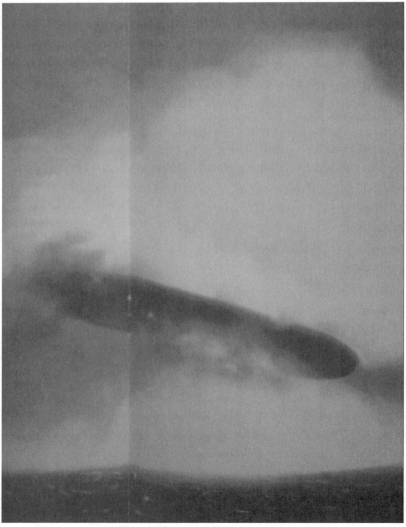

Photo 8 from the USS *Trepang*.

different object.

The next photo shows what appears to be the second object now viewed from behind or edge-on, and it now has the appearance of a roughly triangular wedge shape. The ocean, reflected sunlight, sky and lighting all appear to be captured at roughly the same time of day in lighting conditions consistent with the previous two photographs. The change in apparent shape is most likely due the rotation of the object about another viewing axis.

The last two photos (eight and nine) do not appear to be of the same object or the same incident. It is a similar, cylindrical object over the ocean, but it has a more strictly cylindrical shape, is in color and the object appears to be surrounded by smoke once again. I think the last photo (#9) is simply a crop of the wider shot, showing the glowing red light near the centerline. This last photo is the most heavily criticized, with many observers claiming there is evidence of Photoshop in the clouds both above and below the object. My observation is that the critics may have a point, but if so, this has nothing to do the other seven photos since I do not agree they are of the same objects or incidents. The last photo has a clear crease as well, which I do not agree is Photoshopped, and what appear to be marks where a staple was removed. This implies it was removed as a paper page from a report, book or magazine, and the photograph was taken of the page.

So what are we left with? In my opinion, the first four photos are of a single object from a single incident, separate from the rest. They appear to be taken through the periscope viewfinder of a naval vessel, possibly the *Trepang* as described in the leakers' emails. I find nothing inconsistent between the images indicating they are not authentic.

The send set of three photos (five, six, seven) also appear to be of one object, but I cannot reconcile the appearance of the photos or shape of the object with the first four photos. For that reason, I believe they are of a separate object and/or incident. They also appear to be taken with a different camera/film combination. I have no plausible explanation of what their subject might be.

The last two photos are actually two different versions of the same photo, in my opinion, pulled from a paper report or book and photographed while laying on a table or desk. Once again I do not believe they are connected to either the objects or incidents depicted in the other two sets of photos. There is some evidence of manipulation on the last photo, but not, in my opinion, of the object itself.

So, my conclusions are that the photos are authentic, with the first set of four being consistent with the story told by Mistretta's source. The second set of three photos appears to be of a different object and different incident, but still appear authentic and both

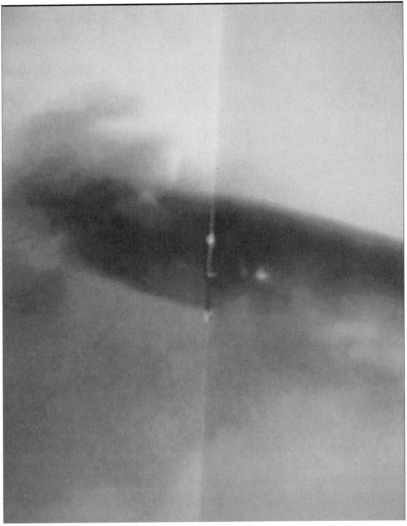

Photo 9 from the USS *Trepang*.

US Navy target blimp.

sets are consistent with photo quality I would expect from the cited (1971) period. The last photos I believe are also most likely authentic, but again from a separate incident not connected to the other two. I think all three sets of USO photos are in fact of real, physical objects.

The question then is, what exactly are they?

It has been suggested that these in fact may simply be photographs of US Navy test target blimps, which were sometimes used during World Wars I and II for target practice for Navy gunners. The problem I have with this explanation is that they don't look like such blimps, they don't perform like blimps (note the rotation) and while there is some smoke around them, indicating they may have been fired at, there is no visible damage from the shooting, which there would be. I also find it hard to reconcile the fact that one of these alleged "blimps" is seen emerging from below the water, certainly not the way such blimps are utilized or deployed. If this were actually a photo of the blimp sinking after being shot down, there would be some evidence of damage, which there is not.

And what are we to make of the evident denials of Sackett and Klika? To me, they are simply expressing plausible denial about incidents they have not been cleared to discuss. So based on these photos alone, I think it's safe to conclude that military encounters with USOs, especially in the late 1960s to early 1970s time period, may be much more numerous than we have thought or ever been told.

Next, we'll look at a completely different kind of USO, one that can still be tested and investigated today.

The Baltic Sea Anomaly

The Baltic Sea anomaly refers to interpretations of a sonar image taken by Peter Lindberg, Dennis Åsberg and their Swedish "Ocean X" diving team while treasure hunting on the floor of the northern Baltic Sea in June 2011. The object was found at the center

A map of the Baltic Sea and the Gulf of Bothnia.

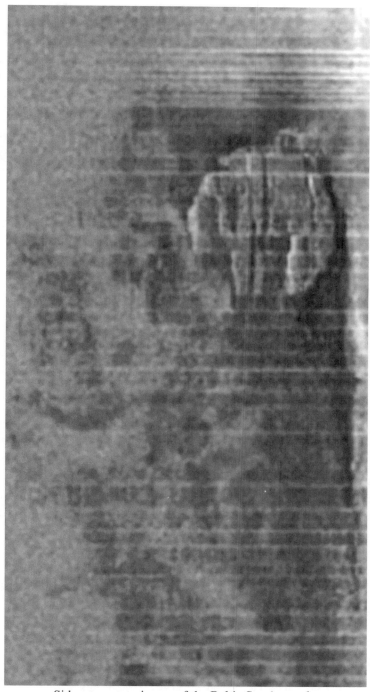

Side-scan sonar image of the Baltic Sea Anomaly.

The "Baltic Sea Anomaly" and the *Millennium Falcon* side by side.

of the Bothnian Sea and immediately caused a controversy as to its nature and origin. The Ocean X team suggested their sonar image showed an object with unusual features of seemingly non-natural origin, prompting speculation published in tabloid newspapers that the object was a sunken UFO (USO). The Swedish-based diving team described themselves as "treasure hunters and salvage operators" that specialize in underwater searches for sunken "antique high-end alcoholic beverages and historic artefacts." According to the team, they returned from an expedition in the Baltic Sea between Sweden and Finland with what they described as a "blurry but interesting" sonar image while searching for an old shipwreck in the summer of 2011.

They claimed that their image shows a 200-foot-diameter circular object found in 300 feet of water with features resembling ramps, stairways, and other structures not produced by nature. Some tabloid news sites made the comparison in shape to the famous *Millennium Falcon* space hot rod from the Star Wars movies; the comparison seemed to fit accurately and caught on. "Han Solo's spaceship found at the bottom of the ocean," the headlines blared. Looking at the side-by-side images, it's easy to see why it captured the public interest. The analogy seems seems apt.

The group revisited the site the following year intending to get a clearer image, but claimed a "mysterious electrical interference" (sound familiar?) knocked out their instruments whenever they got within about 700 feet of the object and prevented them from getting better pictures. Unlike the electronic fog phenomena encountered by so many in the Bermuda Triangle however, in this case the interference seemed to be generated by the object itself, rather than being a side effect of the geologic region in which it resides. I, for one, find it interesting that this "electronic fog" effect didn't seem to occur at the location on the first observation but only on subsequent attempts to re-image and confirm the object on site.

Speculation that it was a wrecked USO or alien spacecraft sprung up immediately after these initial reports, and there were numerous artistic interpretations based on the descriptions of the Ocean X divers who had tried to get near it. They described a metallic, smooth finished surface, quite unlike what would be found on an ancient stone structure or natural rock formation.

This speculation caused an immediate blowback from the scientific community and media gatekeepers, who were quick to respond with headlines claiming that "experts" had reached a consensus that it was a natural object. When, in fact, do such unnamed "experts" not reach such a conclusion? They also were quick to attack the integrity of the Ocean X team: "Jonathan Hill of the Mars Space Flight Facility questioned the motives involved in Ocean X announcements, which included plans to take wealthy tourists in a submarine to visit the site.

Hill was quoted as saying, "Whenever people make extraordinary claims, it's always a good idea to consider for a moment whether they are personally benefiting from the claim or if it's a truly objective observation." He also suggested that it would have been simple to break off a piece and have it geologically tested, and said that test results showing it was simply rock would

The Baltic Sea Anomaly as interpreted from Ocean X diver descriptions (Vaghauk).

173

not have benefited Peter Lindberg.[3] (Of course, scientists who financially benefit from preserving the status quo and their own funding are always above reproach.)

Yet, Lindberg then attempted to do just exactly what Hill suggested he wouldn't. According to sources, samples of stone recovered at the site on the second expedition by Ocean X were given to Volker Brüchert, an associate professor of geology at Stockholm University. Although Ocean X was quick to point out that they were taken *near* the site, not actually from the object itself, mainstream sources quickly seized on Brüchert's analysis. He concluded that the samples indicated that most are granites, gneisses and sandstones, among other natural rocks. Among the samples was also a single loose piece of basaltic (volcanic) rock, which is out of place on the seafloor, but not unusual. Explained Brüchert:

> Because the whole northern Baltic region is so heavily influenced by glacial thawing processes, both the feature and the rock samples are likely to have formed in connection with glacial and postglacial processes. *Possibly* these rocks were transported there by glaciers.

But what most of the news sites who quickly labeled the formation "debunked" failed to mention was that Brüchert only *suspected* the samples were volcanic or glacial, he could not *prove* it.

"I was surprised. When I researched the material I found a great black stone that *could* be a volcanic rock," is what Brüchert actually said. "My *hypothesis* is that this object, this structure, was formed during the Ice Age many thousands of years ago" [emphasis mine]. Swedish geologists Fredrik Klingberg and Martin Jakobsson also saw the samples and claimed that the chemical composition of the samples provided resembles that of nodules that are not uncommon in seabeds, and that the materials found, including limonite and goethite, can indeed be formed by nature itself.

The problem is that the samples aren't actually of the object, but rather were found nearby. None of the "debunking" sources

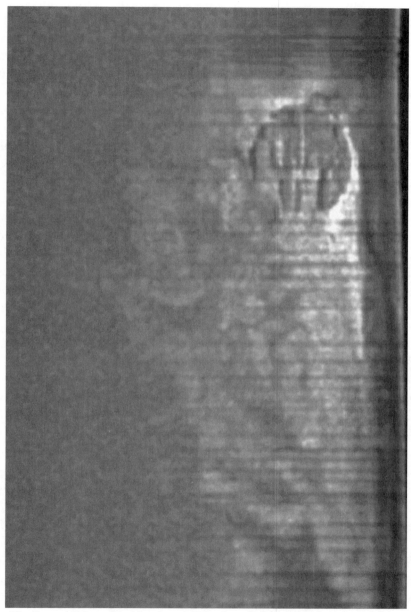

The "trench" first noted by Ocean X in the original side-scan sonar image.

mention that.

Having failed to score a knockout with the sample analysis, critics then turned their attention to the initial sonar image itself.

Hanumant Singh of the Woods Hole Oceanographic Institution has said that the image cannot be trusted because several distortions render it "virtually useless for identifying an undersea formation." According to Singh, the distortions are due to "a cheap inaccurate sonar instrument that was improperly wired and calibrated." He provided no proof to back up his statement. An MSNBC report speculated that interpretations of the image as a flying saucer are likely the result of graphic outlines intended to suggest the fictional spaceship *Millennium Falcon* drawn onto the sonar image by tabloid newspapers. One of the worst Fake News outlets of the last five years, Fake News MSNBC provided once again no evidence whatsoever to support this claim.[4] A simple visual examination of the original sonar image shows that it is neither blurry, indistinct nor "useless for identifying an undersea formation." It is of comparable quality to other sonar images of natural seafloor formations and shipwrecks, and without even a small amount of processing it shows what is clearly a highly unusual object on the ocean floor. Singh is a liar, pure and simple.

This didn't stop the onslaught of attacks. Scientist Charles Paull of the Monterey Bay Aquarium Research Institute told *Popular Mechanics* that the sonar image was more likely of a rock outcrop, sediment dropped from a fishing trawler, or even a school of fish. Paull characterized the story as "curious and fun, but much ado about nothing." Others quickly contradicted that interpretation. Reacting to a photo published by Swedish newspaper *Expressen* purportedly taken by Ocean X during a dive to collect the rock samples, Göran Ekberg, marine archaeologist at Sjöhistoriska museet (Maritime Museum) in Stockholm said, "A natural, geological formation can't be ruled out. I agree the finding looks weird since it's completely circular. But nature has produced stranger things than that." Of course, he failed to provide an example. Martin Jakobsson, professor of marine geology and geophysics at Stockholm University also examined the image and was at least careful in his analysis, He said, "I'm guessing it's some sort of sandstone. But to make things clear, I've only seen the media images, and I need more material before making an official statement."[5] Other "experts" said the image quite possibly shows a grouping of rocks deposited by Ice Age glaciers, or maybe pillow basalt or a moraine.

But the whole "glacial recession" explanation fell apart when better processing was done on the sonar scan showing a miles-long trench carved by the Baltic Sea Anomaly (BSA) along the sefloor. This effectively "rubbished" (as the British would say) the notion that it was formed in place by melting glaciers (which, by the way, can be used to describe practically any feature in the solar system). This trench could only have been formed if the anomaly struck the ocean floor at an angle, a high rate of speed, remained basically intact, and then skidded along the ocean floor for several miles before coming to a rest where the Ocean X team eventually found it.

This means that the samples that were examined and interpreted to be "rocks" where most likely from the surrounding ocean floor and not the object itself, which must be made out of something extraordinary and incredibly hard to have survived such an impact basically intact. The trench also safely discounts the notion, put forth by the Russian newspaper *Pravda*, that it is a concrete footing sunk by Germans in World War II as the base for an anti-submarine net.

Increasingly desperate attempts by the mainstream science community to maintain the conventional explanations have now resorted to claiming that the trench itself, which essentially proves the object was flying when it hit the water, are also the result of receding glaciers which just happened to leave a mark leading right up to the location of the anomaly itself, and then stopping. Their steadfast refusal to admit the obvious, that the BSA *created* the trench when it scraped along the ocean floor, shows that they are simply too locked into their positions to admit the truth, even if it stares them directly in the face.

The Baltic Sea Anomaly is a prime example of an ancient (possibly 140,000 years old) but verifiable USO. All that remains is the difficult task of direct sampling of the object itself to determine if it is in fact a natural, or as seems more likely, a manufactured object. But the question remains, if it turns out to be manufactured,

177

how many more such ancient, impossible "wrecks" must lie beneath our seas, not just in the Triangle itself, but probably all over the world?

Teotihuacan and the Cuban Ruins

Teotihuacan was a major megalithic complex founded around 100 BC by the pre-Columbian civilization that flourished around the time of the Mayans in central Mexico. Dominated by the massive Pyramid of the Sun and lesser Pyramid of the Moon connected along the north-south Avenue of the Dead, it was a huge city for its time, housing at least 125,000 people at its peak. Sometimes associated with the Mayans and at other times with the Aztecs, the entire complex is laid out in relation to various astronomical alignments including its primary siting directly along the magical "19.5°" parallel it shares with the southern boundary of the Bermuda Triangle. Many others have covered the layout and history of the complex in far greater detail than I wish to, but again I think it is a significant site because, like the Martian ruins discovered by Hoagland and decoded by Torun, it seems to have embedded in its alignments an understanding of the significance of the parallel, and its role in the hyperdimensional physics model which I believe drives the atmospheric anomalies encountered by travelers through the Triangle. Interest in its location and placement in relation to the Triangle has only increased in recent years with the discovery of yet another megalithic site along the parallel, one much closer to and even more significant to the mystery of the Triangle itself.

What is today referred to as "The Cuban Underwater City" is a submerged granite structural complex off the coast of the Guanahacabibes Peninsula in the Pinar del Río Province of Cuba. It, like the Baltic Sea Anomaly, was discovered in sonar images in 2001 by Pauline Zalitzki, a marine engineer, and her husband Paul Weinzweig, owners of a Canadian company called Advanced Digital Communications. They spotted symmetrical and geometric stone structures resembling an urban complex covering an area of 1.25 square miles at depths of between 2,000 and 2,500 feet. Zalitzki and Weinzweig made the discovery while working on an underwater survey contract with the Cuban government, who

The Cuban Underwater City (ADC).

had hired ADC to survey for possible oil fields. They were not looking for archeological sites and came upon the complex purely by chance.

After the discovery was first reported, the team received permission to return to the site a second time with an underwater video robot that filmed sonar images interpreted as various pyramids and circular structures made out of massive, smooth blocks of stone that resembled hewn granite. Zalitzki was quoted as saying, "It's a really wonderful structure which really looks like it could have been a large urban center. However, it would be totally irresponsible to say what it was before we have more evidence."

As with the Baltic Sea Anomaly, mainstream scientists were quick to attack the findings on various grounds. After studying the images, *National Geographic* senior editor John Echave said:

> They are interesting anomalies, but that's as much as anyone can say right now. But I'm no expert on sonar and until we are able to actually go down there and see, it will be difficult to characterize them.

University of Rhode Island professor of oceanography Robert Ballard was quoted as saying:

> That's too deep. I'd be surprised if it was human. You have to ask yourself: how did it get there? I've looked at a lot of sonar images in my life, and it can be sort of like looking at an inkblot—people can sometimes see what they want to see. I'll just wait for a bit more data.

Cuban Marine geologist Manuel Iturralde called for more samples before drawing conclusions about the site, saying the results thus far were very unusual. He estimated that it would have taken 50,000 years for such structures to have sunken to the depth at which they were said to be found and stated that none of the known cultures living that long ago had the ability to build such structures. A specialist in underwater archaeology at Florida State University added:

> It would be cool if they were right, but it would be real advanced for anything we would see in the New World for that time frame. The structures are out of time and out of place.

Of course, a good scientist wouldn't let those assumptions— and that's what they are—preclude him from studying such an extraordinary find further. Just because we don't believe that such structures *could* have been built by a human civilization 50,000 years ago doesn't mean they weren't, nor does it preclude some cataclysmic sinking of the continental shelf messing up the timeline. But they won't go there. That would mean bringing the "A" word, Atlantis, into the conversation. Grenville Draper of Florida International was quick to attack the idea stating, "Nothing of this magnitude has been reported, even from the Mediterranean..." Of course, his statement is completely at odds with the mere existence of the Atlantis mythology, which demonstrably does exist.

If the legend of Atlantis doesn't constitute a "report" of cataclysmic tectonic upheavals, exactly what does? I myself

The USS *Scorpion* (SSN-589).

am more interested in the Cuban discovery because of its siting on the 19.5° parallel and its proximity to the boundaries of the Triangle than I am about its possible connection to the Atlantis legend. I suspect there are many such complexes to be discovered all throughout the region of the Triangle, and I suspect we will make mind-shattering discoveries about our own true history from exploring them.

Before we move forward to our conclusions, I think it's important to look at one last case, a case where the association of the underwater ruins, USOs and the mystery of the Triangle all come together: The disappearance of the USS *Scorpion*.

The USS *Scorpion* (SSN-589) was a Skipjack-class nuclear submarine of the United States Navy and the sixth vessel of the US Navy to carry that designation. *Scorpion* was lost on or around the 22nd of May 1968, with 99 crewmen dying in the incident. USS *Scorpion* is one of only two nuclear submarines the US Navy has lost, the other being USS *Thresher*. The *Scorpion*'s keel was laid down August 20, 1958 by General Dynamics Electric Boat in Groton, Connecticut. She was launched December 19, 1959, sponsored by Mrs. Elizabeth S. Morrison, the daughter of the last commander of the World War II-era USS *Scorpion* (SS-278) (which was also lost with all hands, in 1944). *Scorpion* was commissioned July 29, 1960, Commander Norman B. Bessac in command. She then set sail and served reliably for the next seven years.

In early 1968, the *Scorpion,* now under the command of Commander Francis Slattery, arrived at the US Naval Shipyards in Norfolk, Virginia for a "refueling overhaul," meaning that her reactor was replaced with a brand new stat-of-the-art S5W nuclear reactor designed to give her improved speed, performance and reliability at sea. According to the stories, after her refit she set sail for the US naval base in Rota, Spain where she performed some check-out maneuvers and then disappeared some 400 miles south of the Azores; she was never heard from again.

The actual story, as I have been told by contacts within the military, is somewhat different.

According to my sources, the US Navy had been having prolonged and significant USO encounters in the Triangle for years. Long suspecting there was an alien base of operations somewhere near the Tongue of the Ocean, the Navy had chosen to refit some of their fast attack submarines (like the *Scorpion*) with new anti-USO weaponry and high-tech detection equipment. The first part of the *Scorpion*'s refit was in Norfolk, yes, but the installation of nuclear attack torpedoes and electromagnetic interference weaponry was

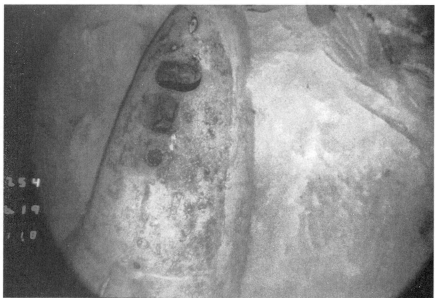

Bow section of the USS *Scorpion* wreck with torpedo room hatch popped open.

completed at a secret naval facility in Carrefour, Haiti. In March of 1968, the *Scorpion* sailed on a course through the Triangle, where she picked up a "stalker," a submerged object which paced the *Scorpion* all over the Caribbean. Officially, the stalker was identified as a Soviet submarine. In truth it was a USO, and never confirmed as a Soviet sub. For an unusually long period, beginning shortly before midnight on May 20th and ending after midnight on May 21st, *Scorpion* attempted to send radio traffic to Naval Station Rota, but was only able to reach a Navy communications station in Nea Makri, Greece, which forwarded *Scorpion's* messages to COMSUBLANT (Commander, Submarine Force Atlantic). A Lt. John Roberts was handed Commander Slattery's last message, that he was closing on the "Soviet submarine and research group," running at a steady 15 knots (17 mph) at a depth of 350 feet "to begin surveillance of the Soviets." Six days later the media reported she was overdue at Norfolk.[6]

In truth what happened is that *Scorpion* received orders from Rota to turn and attack the USO which had been shadowing her, and fired at least one of her nuclear-tipped Mark 45 torpedoes at the unknown. In return, the USO moved through the water at incredible speed, as if it wasn't even submerged, closed on the nose of the *Scorpion*, and unleashed an electromagnetic pulse-type weapon which shut down all the electrical systems on the vessel, and shut down her brand new S5W nuclear reactor. Powerless, the submarine sank until she hit crush depth, broke apart, and ended up at the bottom of the ocean in 10,000 feet of water.

This true sequence of events was later used in the James Cameron feature film *The Abyss* as the movie's opening action sequence. What is depicted is essentially what happened in real life.

A secret search was immediately launched for the vessel, followed by a public search which commenced more than a week later. According to my source, the Navy knew all along what had happened and as soon as the wreck was located, an attempt was made to recover the remaining nuclear-tipped torpedo. This effort, too, encountered "outside interference" and, given the depth of over 10,000 feet, the whole salvage mission was called off. Later, special high-tech submersibles dove the wreck and got some

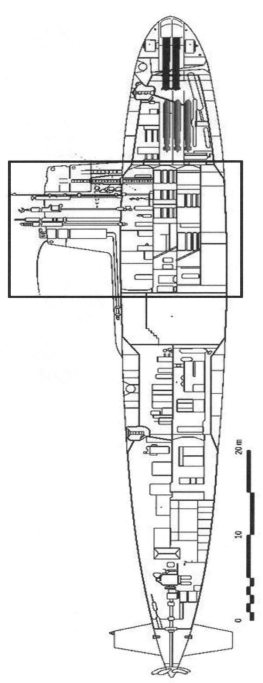

Drawing of the USS *Scorpion* with the missing section marked by the outline.

intriguing pictures. As in *The Abyss*, the forward torpedo room hatch was sprung from the hydrostatic pressure.

But the oddest thing, only recently reported, is that the entire middle section of ship, the operations compartment containing the bridge, conning tower and the new high-technology "avionics" of the ship, was simply *missing*. Officially, this section of the ship was crushed by the pressure below 1,500 feet depth. But the submersibles found no pieces of it at all. It was, as my source stated it, "as if the center section of the boat was simply plucked from the rest of the ship."

The Navy Board of Inquiry, chaired by Vice Admiral Bernard L. Austin, examined many possible causes for the loss of the *Scorpion* but ultimately concluded that, "The certain cause of the loss of the *Scorpion* cannot be ascertained from evidence now available."[7]

Other theories are that the *Scorpion* ran afoul of Soviet submarines on a classified mission. The book *All Hands Down* by Kenneth Sewell and Jerome Preisler (Simon and Schuster, 2008) concludes that the *Scorpion* was destroyed while en route to gather intelligence on a Soviet naval group conducting operations in the Atlantic. While the mission for which the submarine was diverted from her original course back to her home port is a matter of record, its details do remain classified.

Ed Offley's book *Scorpion Down* promotes a hypothesis suggesting that the *Scorpion* was sunk by a Soviet submarine during a standoff that started days before May 22nd. Offley also cites that it occurred roughly at the time of the submarine's intelligence-gathering mission, from which she was redirected from her original heading for home. According to Offley, the flotilla had just been harassed by another US submarine, USS *Haddo*.

Both *All Hands Down* and *Scorpion Down* point toward the involvement of the KGB spy ring (the so-called Walker Spy Ring) led by John Anthony Walker Jr. in the heart of the US Navy's communications, stating that it could have known that *Scorpion* was coming to investigate the Soviet flotilla. According to this theory, both navies agreed to hide the truth about these incidents.

The Navy court of inquiry official statement was that there was

A waterspout in the vicinity of the Florida Keys (NOAA).

not another ship within 200 miles of *Scorpion* at the time of the sinking. Adding to the body of evidence against a Soviet-torpedo-attack theory, US Navy submarine Captain Robert LaGassa has flatly stated that, "no Soviet submarine in 1968 could detect, track, approach and attack any Skipjack or later class US submarine."

I concur with both those assessments. There was no way that the Soviet Navy of the day could have tracked and sunk an advanced, refitted sub like the *Scorpion*. And as my source related "it is true there was no other ship within 200 miles of the *Scorpion*."

Because, it wasn't a ship at all...

Now, while the wreck of the USS *Scorpion* does not technically lay within the accepted boundaries of the Triangle, but rather in the adjacent Sargasso Sea, what I find fascinating is exactly where the wreck, and the possible USO encounter that caused it, did in fact occur. That location is t 32°54.9′N x 33°08.89′W. In other words, 33° X 33°, or pretty much exactly where I would expect a confrontation between a US Navy sub and a hyperdimensionally sensitized, otherworldly USO to confront each other.

I do not think this is an accident. I think this encounter took place at the exact location where the physics dictated it take place, and I think the specially refit US submarine lost the battle because the crew didn't understand that their already technologically superior opponent was drawing even more energy from the grid around it than the Navy anticipated. My final conclusion, based on public facts and what I have been told, is that the sinking of the USS *Scorpion* is the first, and as far as I know only, direct attack in the Bermuda Triangle by an otherworldly technology on a US military target.

May the officers and crew of the *Scorpion* now rest in peace.

(Endnotes)

1 https://www.theblackvault.com/casefiles/arctic-ufo-photographs-uss-trepang-ssn-674-march-1971/#

2 https://www.theblackvault.com/casefiles/wp-content/up-loads/2015/07/trepangroster.pdf

3 https://en.wikipedia.org/wiki/Baltic_Sea_anomaly

4 https://www.livescience.com/22846-mysterious-baltic-sea-object-is-a-glacial-deposit.html

5 https://www.expressen.se/nyheter/trappa-senaste-fyndet-vid-mystiska-cirkeln/

6 https://en.wikipedia.org/wiki/USS_Scorpion_(SSN-589)

7 "Loss of Scorpion Baffles Inquiry," *New York Times*, February 1, 1969, pp. 1, 14.

A Mayan frieze from Copan in the Yucatan showing the destruction of a pyramid, a volcano erupting, and man drowning and a man escaping in a boat.

Chapter 7

Summation

As we have now seen, in my opinion there are many cases which raise significant and worthwhile questions about the reality of the Bermuda Triangle mystery. From the early seagoing vessels which simply disappeared in good weather or ran aground without their crews, we have advanced the issues raised all the way to a missing nuclear-armed submarine that was somehow stalked and sank in or near the Bermuda Triangle. We have added cases to the enigma and shed new light on the classic cases, like the "outer space" ham radio revelation about Flight 19. We have popped the

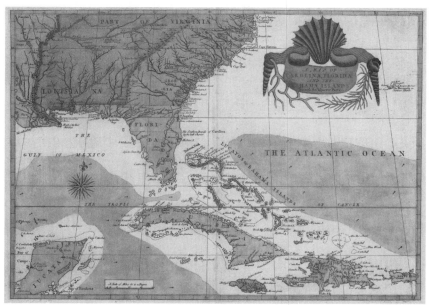

An old map of Florida, Cuba and the Bahamas.

hatch on the case of the USS *Scorpion*, upon which a Hollywood film was based. We have shed new light (with the help of Quasar) on the case of the missing Operation Sky Shield II B-52 bomber, which is kind of hard to lose. We have looked into the mystery of Bruce Gernon's harrowing encounter with the Triangle's hyperdimensional fog, and recognized that he may be the only person to have survived it. Lastly, we have delved into the actual physics of the Triangle, which may have finally unlocked why the area is so volatile, and seems to exist partially in the netherworld between this dimension and next, wherever that is.

Looking at all these cases, we must acknowledge the possibility that all of these lost souls are still alive in some timeless, parallel universe somewhere. Maybe the middle section of the *Scorpion* was "plucked" out of the sub in order to save the crew, to rescue them from an attempted interdimensional communication gone wrong. Maybe the pilots of Flight 19 are still out there, trying to find their way home and not realizing 75 years have passed.

By connecting the physics of the Triangle with the physics that the Monuments of Mars led us to decode decades ago, we now have some basis going forward to look at these cases in a different way, to consider a very real possibility that answers may yet be found to the mystery of what happened.

At least, until the next mystery of the Triangle emerges from either the ashes of history, or a more hopeful and better-prepared future.

Mike Bara

A waterspout off of Punta Gorda, Florida (NOAA).

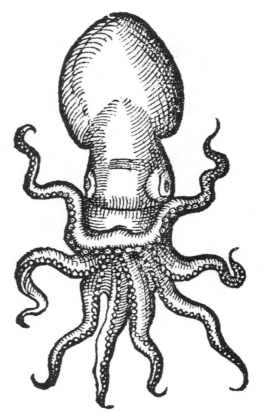

Beware the Kraken.

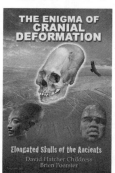
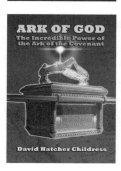

BIGFOOT NATION
A History of Sasquatch in North America
By David Hatcher Childress
Childress takes a deep look at Bigfoot Nation—the real world of bigfoot around us in the United States and Canada. Whether real or imagined, that bigfoot has made his way into the American psyche cannot be denied. He appears in television commercials, movies, and on roadside billboards. Bigfoot is everywhere, with actors portraying him in variously believable performances and it has become the popular notion that bigfoot is both dangerous and horny. Indeed, bigfoot is out there stalking lovers' lanes and is even more lonely than those frightened teenagers that he sometimes interrupts. Bigfoot, tall and strong as he is, makes a poor leading man in the movies with his awkward personality and typically anti-social behavior. Includes 16-pages of color photos that document Bigfoot Nation!
320 Pages. 6x9 Paperback. Illustrated. $22.00. Code: BGN

MEN & GODS IN MONGOLIA
by Henning Haslund
Haslund takes us to the lost city of Karakota in the Gobi desert. We meet the Bodgo Gegen, a god-king in Mongolia similar to the Dalai Lama of Tibet. We meet Dambin Jansang, the dreaded warlord of the "Black Gobi." Haslund and companions journey across the Gobi desert by camel caravan; are kidnapped and held for ransom; witness initiation into Shamanic societies; meet reincarnated warlords; and experience the violent birth of "modern" Mongolia.
358 Pages. 6x9 Paperback. Illustrated. $18.95. Code: MGM

PROJECT MK-ULTRA
AND MIND CONTROL TECHNOLOGY
By Axel Balthazar
This book is a compilation of the government's documentation on MK-Ultra, the CIA's mind control experimentation on unwitting human subjects, as well as over 150 patents pertaining to artificial telepathy (voice-to-skull technology), behavior modification through radio frequencies, directed energy weapons, electronic monitoring, implantable nanotechnology, brain wave manipulation, nervous system manipulation, neuroweapons, psychological warfare, satellite terrorism, subliminal messaging, and more. A must-have reference guide for targeted individuals and anyone interested in the subject of mind control technology.
384 pages. 7x10 Paperback. Illustrated. $19.95. Code: PMK

LIQUID CONSPIRACY 2:
The CIA, MI6 & Big Pharma's War on Psychedelics
By Xaviant Haze
Underground author Xaviant Haze looks into the CIA and its use of LSD as a mind control drug; at one point every CIA officer had to take the drug and endure mind control tests and interrogations to see if the drug worked as a "truth serum." Chapters include: The Pioneers of Psychedelia; The United Kingdom Mellows Out: The MI5, MDMA and LSD; Taking it to the Streets: LSD becomes Acid; Great Works of Art Inspired and Influenced by Acid; Scapolamine: The CIA's Ultimate Truth Serum; Mind Control, the Death of Music and the Meltdown of the Masses; Big Pharma's War on Psychedelics; The Healing Powers of Psychedelic Medicine; tons more.
240 pages. 6x9 Paperback. Illustrated. $19.95. Code: LQC2

ANCIENT ALIENS AND JFK
The Race to the Moon & the Kennedy Assassination
By Mike Bara
Relying on never-before-seen documents culled from the recent Kennedy assassination papers document dump, Bara shows the secret connections between key assassination figures like Oswald, LBJ, and highly placed figures inside NASA who had reasons to want Kennedy dead. Bara also looks into the bizarre billion-dollar Treasury bonds that Japanese businessmen attempted to deposit in a Swiss bank that had photos of Kennedy and the Moon on them. Is the wealth of the Moon being used as collateral by the USA? The book will dig deeply into Kennedy's silent war with shadowy Deep State figures who were desperate to shut down his Disclosure agenda. Also: the Apollo mission; "Apollo 20," and more. Includes 8-page color section.
248 Pages. 6x9 Paperback. Illustrated. $19.95. Code: AAJK

HIDDEN AGENDA
NASA and the Secret Space Program
By Mike Bara
Bara delves into secret bases on the Moon, and exploring the many other rumors surrounding the military's secret projects in space. On June 8, 1959, a group at the ABMA produced for the US Department of the Army a report entitled Project Horizon, a "Study for the Establishment of a Lunar Military Outpost." The permanent outpost was predicted to cost $6 billion and was to become operational in December 1966 with twelve soldiers stationed at the Moon base. Did NASA and the Pentagon expect to find evidence of alien bases on the Moon? Does hacker Gary Mackinnon's discovery of defense department documents identifying "non-terrestrial officers" serving in space mean that the US has secret space platforms designed to fight a war with an alien race? Includes an 8-page color section.
346 Pages. 6x9 Paperback. Illustrated. $19.95. Code: HDAG

MIND CONTROL, OSWALD & JFK
Introduction by Kenn Thomas
In 1969 the strange book Were We Controlled? was published which maintained that Lee Harvey Oswald was a special agent who was also a Mind Control subject who had received an implant in 1960. Thomas examines the evidence that Oswald had been an early recipient of the Mind Control implant technology and this startling role in the JFK Assassination. Also: the RHIC-EDOM Mind Control aspects concerning the RFK assassination and the history of implant technology.
256 Pages. 6x9 Paperback. Illustrated. $16.00. Code: MCOJ

ADVENTURES OF A HASHISH SMUGGLER
by Henri de Monfreid
Nobleman, writer, adventurer and inspiration for the swashbuckling gun runner in the Adventures of Tintin, Henri de Monfreid lived by his own account "a rich, restless, magnificent life" as one of the great travelers of his or any age. The son of a French artist who knew Paul Gaugin as a child, de Monfreid sought his fortune by becoming a collector and merchant of the fabled Persian Gulf pearls. He was then drawn into the shadowy world of arms trading, slavery, smuggling and drugs. Infamous as well as famous, his name is inextricably linked to the Red Sea and the raffish ports between Suez and Aden in the early years of the twentieth century. De Monfreid (1879 to 1974) had a long life of many adventures around the Horn of Africa where he dodged pirates as well as the authorities.
284 Pages. 6x9 Paperback. $16.95. Illustrated. Code AHS

TECHNOLOGY OF THE GODS
The Incredible Sciences of the Ancients
by David Hatcher Childress

Childress looks at the technology that was allegedly used in Atlantis and the theory that the Great Pyramid of Egypt was originally a gigantic power station. He examines tales of ancient flight and the technology that it involved; how the ancients used electricity; megalithic building techniques; the use of crystal lenses and the fire from the gods; evidence of various high tech weapons in the past, including atomic weapons; ancient metallurgy and heavy machinery; the role of modern inventors such as Nikola Tesla in bringing ancient technology back into modern use; impossible artifacts; and more.

356 pages. 6x9 Paperback. Illustrated. $16.95. code: TGOD

THE ANTI-GRAVITY HANDBOOK
edited by David Hatcher Childress

The new expanded compilation of material on Anti-Gravity, Free Energy, Flying Saucer Propulsion, UFOs, Suppressed Technology, NASA Cover-ups and more. Highly illustrated with patents, technical illustrations and photos. This revised and expanded edition has more material, including photos of Area 51, Nevada, the government's secret testing facility. This classic on weird science is back in a new format!

230 PAGES. 7x10 PAPERBACK. ILLUSTRATED. $16.95. CODE: AGH

ANTI-GRAVITY & THE WORLD GRID

Is the earth surrounded by an intricate electromagnetic grid network offering free energy? This compilation of material on ley lines and world power points contains chapters on the geography, mathematics, and light harmonics of the earth grid. Learn the purpose of ley lines and ancient megalithic structures located on the grid. Discover how the grid made the Philadelphia Experiment possible. Explore the Coral Castle and many other mysteries, including acoustic levitation, Tesla Shields and scalar wave weaponry. Browse through the section on anti-gravity patents, and research resources.

274 PAGES. 7x10 PAPERBACK. ILLUSTRATED. $14.95. CODE: AGW

ANTI-GRAVITY & THE UNIFIED FIELD
edited by David Hatcher Childress

Is Einstein's Unified Field Theory the answer to all of our energy problems? Explored in this compilation of material is how gravity, electricity and magnetism manifest from a unified field around us. Why artificial gravity is possible; secrets of UFO propulsion; free energy; Nikola Tesla and anti-gravity airships of the 20s and 30s; flying saucers as superconducting whirls of plasma; anti-mass generators; vortex propulsion; suppressed technology; government cover-ups; gravitational pulse drive; spacecraft & more.

240 PAGES. 7x10 PAPERBACK. ILLUSTRATED. $14.95. CODE: AGU

THE TIME TRAVEL HANDBOOK
A Manual of Practical Teleportation & Time Travel
edited by David Hatcher Childress

The Time Travel Handbook takes the reader beyond the government experiments and deep into the uncharted territory of early time travellers such as Nikola Tesla and Guglielmo Marconi and their alleged time travel experiments, as well as the Wilson Brothers of EMI and their connection to the Philadelphia Experiment—the U.S. Navy's forays into invisibility, time travel, and teleportation. Childress looks into the claims of time travelling individuals, and investigates the unusual claim that the pyramids on Mars were built in the future and sent back in time. A highly visual, large format book, with patents, photos and schematics. Be the first on your block to build your own time travel device!

316 PAGES. 7x10 PAPERBACK. ILLUSTRATED. $16.95. CODE: TTH

ANCIENT ALIENS ON THE MOON
By Mike Bara
What did NASA find in their explorations of the solar system that they may have kept from the general public? How ancient really are these ruins on the Moon? Using official NASA and Russian photos of the Moon, Bara looks at vast cityscapes and domes in the Sinus Medii region as well as glass domes in the Crisium region. Bara also takes a detailed look at the mission of Apollo 17 and the case that this was a salvage mission, primarily concerned with investigating an opening into a massive hexagonal ruin near the landing site. Chapters include: The History of Lunar Anomalies; The Early 20th Century; Sinus Medii; To the Moon Alice!; Mare Crisium; Yes, Virginia, We Really Went to the Moon; Apollo 17; more. Tons of photos of the Moon examined for possible structures and other anomalies.
248 Pages. 6x9 Paperback. Illustrated.. $19.95. Code: AAOM

ANCIENT ALIENS ON MARS
By Mike Bara
Bara brings us this lavishly illustrated volume on alien structures on Mars. Was there once a vast, technologically advanced civilization on Mars, and did it leave evidence of its existence behind for humans to find eons later? Did these advanced extraterrestrial visitors vanish in a solar system wide cataclysm of their own making, only to make their way to Earth and start anew? Was Mars once as lush and green as the Earth, and teeming with life? Chapters include: War of the Worlds; The Mars Tidal Model; The Death of Mars; Cydonia and the Face on Mars; The Monuments of Mars; The Search for Life on Mars; The True Colors of Mars and The Pathfinder Sphinx; more. Color section.
252 Pages. 6x9 Paperback. Illustrated. $19.95. Code: AMAR

ANCIENT ALIENS ON MARS II
By Mike Bara
Using data acquired from sophisticated new scientific instruments like the Mars Odyssey THEMIS infrared imager, Bara shows that the region of Cydonia overlays a vast underground city full of enormous structures and devices that may still be operating. He peels back the layers of mystery to show images of tunnel systems, temples and ruins, and exposes the sophisticated NASA conspiracy designed to hide them. Bara also tackles the enigma of Mars' hollowed out moon Phobos, and exposes evidence that it is artificial. Long-held myths about Mars, including claims that it is protected by a sophisticated UFO defense system, are examined. Data from the Mars rovers Spirit, Opportunity and Curiosity are examined; everything from fossilized plants to mechanical debris is exposed in images taken directly from NASA's own archives.
294 Pages. 6x9 Paperback. Illustrated. $19.95. Code: AAM2

ANCIENT TECHNOLOGY IN PERU & BOLIVIA
By David Hatcher Childress
Childress speculates on the existence of a sunken city in Lake Titicaca and reveals new evidence that the Sumerians may have arrived in South America 4,000 years ago. He demonstrates that the use of "keystone cuts" with metal clamps poured into them to secure megalithic construction was an advanced technology used all over the world, from the Andes to Egypt, Greece and Southeast Asia. He maintains that only power tools could have made the intricate articulation and drill holes found in extremely hard granite and basalt blocks in Bolivia and Peru, and that the megalith builders had to have had advanced methods for moving and stacking gigantic blocks of stone, some weighing over 100 tons.
340 Pages. 6x9 Paperback. Illustrated.. $19.95 Code: ATP

HESS AND THE PENGUINS
The Holocaust, Antarctica and the Strange Case of Rudolf Hess
By Joseph P. Farrell
Farrell looks at Hess' mission to make peace with Britain and get rid of Hitler—even a plot to fly Hitler to Britain for capture! How much did Göring and Hitler know of Rudolf Hess' subversive plot, and what happened to Hess? Why was a doppleganger put in Spandau Prison and then "suicided"? Did the British use an early form of mind control on Hess' double? John Foster Dulles of the OSS and CIA suspected as much. Farrell also uncovers the strange death of Admiral Richard Byrd's son in 1988, about the same time of the death of Hess.
288 Pages. 6x9 Paperback. Illustrated. $19.95. Code: HAPG

HIDDEN FINANCE, ROGUE NETWORKS & SECRET SORCERY
The Fascist International, 9/11, & Penetrated Operations
By Joseph P. Farrell
Farrell investigates the theory that there were not *two* levels to the 9/11 event, but *three*. He says that the twin towers were downed by the force of an exotic energy weapon, one similar to the Tesla energy weapon suggested by Dr. Judy Wood, and ties together the tangled web of missing money, secret technology and involvement of portions of the Saudi royal family. Farrell unravels the many layers behind the 9-11 attack, layers that include the Deutschebank, the Bush family, the German industrialist Carl Duisberg, Saudi Arabian princes and the energy weapons developed by Tesla before WWII.
296 Pages. 6x9 Paperback. Illustrated. $19.95. Code: HFRN

THRICE GREAT HERMETICA & THE JANUS AGE
By Joseph P. Farrell
What do the Fourth Crusade, the exploration of the New World, secret excavations of the Holy Land, and the pontificate of Innocent the Third all have in common? Answer: Venice and the Templars. What do they have in common with Jesus, Gottfried Leibniz, Sir Isaac Newton, Rene Descartes, and the Earl of Oxford? Answer: Egypt and a body of doctrine known as Hermeticism. The hidden role of Venice and Hermeticism reached far and wide, into the plays of Shakespeare (a.k.a. Edward DeVere, Earl of Oxford), into the quest of the three great mathematicians of the Early Enlightenment for a lost form of analysis, and back into the end of the classical era, to little known Egyptian influences at work during the time of Jesus.
354 Pages. 6x9 Paperback. Illustrated. $19.95. Code: TGHJ

ROBOT ZOMBIES
Transhumanism and the Robot Revolution
By Xaviant Haze and Estrella Eguino,
Technology is growing exponentially and the moment when it merges with the human mind, called "The Singularity," is visible in our imminent future. Science and technology are pushing forward, transforming life as we know it—perhaps even giving humans a shot at immortality. Who will benefit from this? This book examines the history and future of robotics, artificial intelligence, zombies and a Transhumanist utopia/dystopia integrating man with machine. Chapters include: Love, Sex and Compassion—Android Style; Humans Aren't Working Like They Used To; Skynet Rises; Blueprints for Transhumans; Kurzweil's Quest; Nanotech Dreams; Zombies Among Us; Cyborgs (Cylons) in Space; Awakening the Human; more. Color Section.
180 Pages. 6x9 Paperback. Illustrated. $16.95. Code: RBTZ

ANCIENT ALIENS & SECRET SOCIETIES
By Mike Bara

Did ancient "visitors"—of extraterrestrial origin—come to Earth long, long ago and fashion man in their own image? Were the science and secrets that they taught the ancients intended to be a guide for all humanity to the present era? Bara establishes the reality of the catastrophe that jolted the human race, and traces the history of secret societies from the priesthood of Amun in Egypt to the Templars in Jerusalem and the Scottish Rite Freemasons. Bara also reveals the true origins of NASA and exposes the bizarre triad of secret societies in control of that agency since its inception. Chapters include: Out of the Ashes; From the Sky Down; Ancient Aliens?; The Dawn of the Secret Societies; The Fractures of Time; Into the 20th Century; The Wink of an Eye; more.

288 Pages. 6x9 Paperback. Illustrated. $19.95. Code: AASS

THE CRYSTAL SKULLS
Astonishing Portals to Man's Past
by David Hatcher Childress and Stephen S. Mehler

Childress introduces the technology and lore of crystals, and then plunges into the turbulent times of the Mexican Revolution form the backdrop for the rollicking adventures of Ambrose Bierce, the renowned journalist who went missing in the jungles in 1913, and F.A. Mitchell-Hedges, the notorious adventurer who emerged from the jungles with the most famous of the crystal skulls. Mehler shares his extensive knowledge of and experience with crystal skulls. Having been involved in the field since the 1980s, he has personally examined many of the most influential skulls, and has worked with the leaders in crystal skull research, including the inimitable Nick Nocerino, who developed a meticulous methodology for the purpose of examining the skulls.

294 pages. 6x9 Paperback. Illustrated. Bibliography. $18.95. Code: CRSK

AXIS OF THE WORLD
The Search for the Oldest American Civilization
by Igor Witkowski

Polish author Witkowski's research reveals remnants of a high civilization that was able to exert its influence on almost the entire planet, and did so with full consciousness. Sites around South America show that this was not just one of the places influenced by this culture, but a place where they built their crowning achievements. Easter Island, in the southeastern Pacific, constitutes one of them. The Rongo-Rongo language that developed there points westward to the Indus Valley. Taken together, the facts presented by Witkowski provide a fresh, new proof that an antediluvian, great civilization flourished several millennia ago.

220 pages. 6x9 Paperback. Illustrated. References. $18.95. Code: AXOW

LEY LINE & EARTH ENERGIES
An Extraordinary Journey into the Earth's Natural Energy System
by David Cowan & Chris Arnold

The mysterious standing stones, burial grounds and stone circles that lace Europe, the British Isles and other areas have intrigued scientists, writers, artists and travellers through the centuries. How do ley lines work? How did our ancestors use Earth energy to map their sacred sites and burial grounds? How do ghosts and poltergeists interact with Earth energy? How can Earth spirals and black spots affect our health? This exploration shows how natural forces affect our behavior, how they can be used to enhance our health and well being.

368 PAGES. 6x9 PAPERBACK. ILLUSTRATED. $18.95. CODE: LLEE

ORDER FORM

10% Discount When You Order 3 or More Items!

One Adventure Place
P.O. Box 74
Kempton, Illinois 60946
United States of America
Tel.: 815-253-6390 • Fax: 815-253-6300
Email: auphq@frontiernet.net
http://www.adventuresunlimitedpress.com

ORDERING INSTRUCTIONS

✓ Remit by USD$ Check, Money Order or Credit Card

✓ Visa, Master Card, Discover & AmEx Accepted

✓ Paypal Payments Can Be Made To:

    info@wexclub.com

✓ Prices May Change Without Notice

✓ 10% Discount for 3 or More Items

SHIPPING CHARGES

United States

✓ Postal Book Rate { $4.50 First Item / 50¢ Each Additional Item

✓ POSTAL BOOK RATE Cannot Be Tracked!
Not responsible for non-delivery.

✓ Priority Mail { $6.00 First Item / $2.00 Each Additional Item

✓ UPS { $7.00 First Item / $1.50 Each Additional Item

NOTE: UPS Delivery Available to Mainland USA Only

Canada

✓ Postal Air Mail { $15.00 First Item / $2.50 Each Additional Item

✓ Personal Checks or Bank Drafts MUST BE

    US$ and Drawn on a US Bank

✓ Canadian Postal Money Orders OK

✓ Payment MUST BE US$

All Other Countries

✓ Sorry, No Surface Delivery!

✓ Postal Air Mail { $19.00 First Item / $6.00 Each Additional Item

✓ Checks and Money Orders MUST BE US$
and Drawn on a US Bank or branch.

✓ Paypal Payments Can Be Made in US$ To:
info@wexclub.com

SPECIAL NOTES

✓ RETAILERS: Standard Discounts Available

✓ BACKORDERS: We Backorder all Out-of-
Stock Items Unless Otherwise Requested

✓ PRO FORMA INVOICES: Available on Request

✓ DVD Return Policy: Replace defective DVDs only

ORDER ONLINE AT: www.adventuresunlimitedpress.com

10% Discount When You Order 3 or More Items!

Please check: ✓

☐ This is my first order   ☐ I have ordered before

Name

Address

City

State/Province   Postal Code

Country

Phone: Day   Evening

Fax   Email

Item Code	Item Description	Qty	Total

Please check: ✓

	Subtotal ▶
	Less Discount-10% for 3 or more items ▶
☐ Postal-Surface	Balance ▶
☐ Postal-Air Mail (Priority in USA)	Illinois Residents 6.25% Sales Tax ▶
	Previous Credit ▶
☐ UPS	Shipping ▶
(Mainland USA only)	Total (check/MO in USD$ only) ▶

☐ Visa/MasterCard/Discover/American Express

Card Number:

Expiration Date: Security Code:

✓ SEND A CATALOG TO A FRIEND: